Ajesh Faizal
Aswathy S U
Roy V I

Professional Ethics in Engineering : an Industry Perspective

Ajesh Faizal
Aswathy S U
Roy V I

Professional Ethics in Engineering : an Industry Perspective

Noor Publishing

Imprint

Any brand names and product names mentioned in this book are subject to trademark, brand or patent protection and are trademarks or registered trademarks of their respective holders. The use of brand names, product names, common names, trade names, product descriptions etc. even without a particular marking in this work is in no way to be construed to mean that such names may be regarded as unrestricted in respect of trademark and brand protection legislation and could thus be used by anyone.

Cover image: www.ingimage.com

Publisher:
Noor Publishing
is a trademark of
International Book Market Service Ltd., member of OmniScriptum Publishing Group
17 Meldrum Street, Beau Bassin 71504, Mauritius
Printed at: see last page
ISBN: 978-620-2-79244-8

Copyright © Ajesh Faizal, Aswathy S U, Roy V I
Copyright © 2021 International Book Market Service Ltd., member of OmniScriptum Publishing Group

PROFESSIONAL ETHICS IN ENGINEERING: AN INDUSTRY PERSPECTIVE

AJESH FAIZAL
Professor, Department of Computer Science and Engineering, Musaliar College of Engineering,
Pathanamthitta, India

ASWATHY S U
Professor, Department of Computer Science and Engineering, Jyothi Engineering College,
Thrissur, India

ROY V I
Professor, Department of Basic Science, Jyothi Engineering College, Thrissur, India

ACKNOWLEDGEMENT

The endless thanks go to The Lord Almighty for all the blessings he has showered onto us, in the process of putting this book together.

We sincerely offer deepest gratitude and thanks to Rev. Fr. Roy Joseph Vadakkan, Secretary & Campus Head, Jyothi Engineering College and Rev. DR. Jose Kannampuzha, Director of Academics, Jyothi Engineering College, Mr. P I Sherief Muhammedh, Chairman, Musaliar Group of Institutions, Prof. Jaya Prasad, Dean, Musalair College of Engineering, Pathanmthitta for their constant guidance and encouragement to accomplish this book.

Also, we would like to thank our colleagues for their support and encouragement that they have given us. It provides us with a great opportunity to look back, and thank to all those who have been directly or indirectly instrumental in successful completion of this book

CONTENTS

(iii)

UNIT -1

ENGINEERING ETHICS

OVERVIEW

Engineering Ethics is the activity and discipline aimed at

(a) understanding the moral values that ought to guide engineering profession or practice,

(b) resolving moral issues in engineering, and

(c) justifying the moral judgments in engineering. It deals with set of moral problems and issues connected with engineering.

Engineering ethics is defined by the codes and standards of conduct endorsed by engineering(professional)societies with respect to the particular set of beliefs, attitudes and habits displayed by the individual or group. Another important goal of engineering ethics is the discovery of the set of justified moral principles of obligation, rights and ideals that ought to be endorsed by the engineers and apply them to concrete situations. Engineering is the largest profession and the decisions and actions of engineers affect all of us in almost all areas of our lives, namely public safety, health, and welfare.

SCOPE

The scopes of engineering ethics are twofold:

1. Ethics of the workplace which involves the co-workers and employees in an organization.

2. Ethics related to the product or work which involves the transportation, warehousing, and use, besides the safety of the end product and the environment outside the factory.

APPROACH

There are conventionally two approaches in the study of ethics:

1. Micro-ethics which deals with decisions and problems of individuals, professionals, and companies.

2. Macro-ethics which deals with the societal problems on a regional/national level. For example, global issues, collective responsibilities of groups such as professional societies and consumer groups.

1.1 SENSES OF ENGINEERING ETHICS

There are two different senses (meanings) of engineering ethics, namely the Normative and the Descriptive senses. The normative sense includes:

(a) Knowing moral values, finding accurate solutions to moral problems and justifying moral judgments in engineering practices,

(b) Study of decisions, policies, and values that are morally desirable in the engineering practice and research, and

1

Using codes of ethics and standards and applying them in their transactions by engineers. The descriptive sense refers to what specific individual or group of engineers believe an act, without justifying their beliefs or actions.

1.2 MORALITY AND MORAL ISSUES

What is morality?
- ✓ The word morality is concerned with:
    - What morally ought or ought not to be given in a given situation;
    - What is morally right or wrong an out the handling of the situation; and/or
    - What is morally good or bad about the people, policies, and ideals involved in it?
- ✓ According to the Oxford dictionary, morality means principles concerning right and wrong or good and bad behavior.
- ✓ Moral reasons are required to support an act (or an ideal) to be called as morally right act (or an ideal is moral)

VARIETY OF MORAL ISSUES

Approaches to engineering ethics. There are two different approaches of engineering ethics.
1. Micro-ethics: this approach addresses typical, everyday problems that the engineers face in their professional life. In other words, micro-ethics describes ethical issues that may affect an engineer 's professional and personal life.
2. Macro-ethics: this approach deals with all societal problems that engineers encounter during their career. In other words, macro-ethics discusses ethical issues concerning all societal problems that engineers might encounter.

Where and how do moral problems arise in engineering? (contexts of professional disagreements faced by engineers). Engineers carry out various activities and decision-making exercises involving technical, financial, managerial, environmental, and ethical issues. There are many situations and moral issues that cause professional disagreements among engineers. The varieties of moral issues are:

1. **Organization oriented issues**
    - ✓ Being an employee to firm, the engineer has to work towards the achievement of the objectives of his/her organization.
    - ✓ Engineers have to give higher priority to the benefits of the organization than one 's own benefits.
    - ✓ Engineers should be able to work collectively with colleagues and other members in order to achieve firm's goals.

2. **Clients or customers-oriented issues**
    - ✓ As we know, the purpose of any business is to reach and satisfy the end users. Therefore, the customers 'requirements should be met.

✓ In this regard, engineers have a major role to play in identifying the _customer voice ', and incorporating the voice of the customer into the product design and manufacture.

✓ Apart from engineering technicality issues, engineers also should face other moral and ethical issues with clients/customers.

3. Competitors oriented issues

✓ In order to withstand in a market, engineers should produce things better than their competitors by all means.

✓ But engineers should not practice cut-throat competition. They should follow certain professional behavior while facing their competitors.

✓ Thus, engineers should hold paramount the safety, health and welfare of the customers in the performance of their professional duties.

4. Law, government and public agencies-oriented issues

✓ The engineers should obey and voluntarily comply with all the governmental rules and regulations related to them.

✓ They should also respect and honestly practice all other similar laws, policies, and regulations.

5. Professional societies-oriented issues

✓ The engineers should follow strictly the various codes of ethics by various professional societies such as National Society of Professional Engineers (NSPE), the Institute of Electrical and Electronics Engineers (IEEE), and American Society of Mechanical Engineers (ASME), in order to perform standard professional behavior.

✓ Professional codes of ethics reflect basic norms 'of conduct that exist within a particular professional and provide general guidance relating to a variety of issues.

6. Social and environmental oriented issues

✓ Since the works of engineers have a direct and vital impact on the quality of life for all people, the engineers should be dedicating to the protection of the public health, safety and welfare.

✓ Also, engineers need to be aware the releasements of experimenters. They should have a united commitment in protecting the environment. They should not involve in any unethical environmental issues such as misusing scarce resources, and fouling environment.

7. Family oriented issues

✓ As a human being and the member of a family, the engineers do have family obligations to take care the needs of their family members. But they should not take any decisions for their own benefits at the cost of public, clients, or employers.

Thus, the above discussion explains how the ethical problems often arise in the engineering profession

1.2 TYPES OF INQUIRIES

1. NORMATIVE INQUIRY

These are about 'what ought to be' and 'what is good'. These questions identify and also justify the morally desirable norms or standards. Some of the questions are:

a. How far engineers are obligated to protect public safety in given situations?
b. When should engineers start whistle blowing on dangerous practices of their employers?
c. Whose values are primary in taking a moral decision, employee, public or govt?
d. Why are engineers obligated to protect public safety?
e. When is govt justified in interfering on such issues and why?

2. CONCEPTUAL INQUIRY

These questions should lead to clarifications on concepts, principles and issues in ethics. Examples are:

a. What is 'SAFETY' and how is it related to' RISK'
b. 'Protect the safety, health and welfare of public'-What does this statement mean?
c. What is a bribe?
d. What is a 'profession' and who are' professionals'?

3. FACTUAL (DESCRIPTIVE) INQUIRIES

These are inquiries used to uncover information using scientific techniques. These inquiries get to information about business realities, history of engineering profession, procedures used in assessment of risks and engineer's psychology.

Why study ENGINEERING ETHICS

ENGINEERING ETHICS is a means to increase the ability of concerned engineers, managers, citizens and others to responsibly confront moral issues raised by technological activities.

1.3 MORAL DILEMMAS

There are three types of complexities.

a. **VAGUENESS**: This complexity arises due to the fact that it is not clear to individuals as to which moral considerations or principles apply to their situation.

b. **CONFLICTING REASONS**: Even when it is perfectly clear as to which moral principle is applicable to one's situation, there could develop a situation where in two or more clearly applicable moral principles come into conflict.

c. **DISAGREEMENT**: Individuals and groups may disagree how to interpret, apply and balance moral reasons in particular situations.

Steps in confronting moral dilemmas

In order to face/overcome the above said moral dilemmas, one can follow one or more of the following steps.

Step 1: Identifying the pertinent moral factors and reasons. It involves addressing solutions for conflicting responsibilities, opposing rights, and incompatible ideals involved.

Step 2: Collecting all the available moral considerations, which are relevant to the moral factors involved

Step 3: Ranking the above collected moral considerations on the basis of importance as applicable to the particular situation.

Step 4: Making factual inquires. In other words, finding alternative courses of actions to resolve the moral dilemmas and following the complete implications of each.

Step 5: Inviting discussions, suggestions from colleagues, friends, and other involved persons to critically examine the moral dilemmas.

Step 6: Taking the final decision. That, is selecting the more reasonable solution by weighing all the relevant moral factors and reasons.

In practice, exercising the above skill to face moral dilemmas is very difficult. The study of engineering ethics helps the engineers to develop and strengthen the skills in resolving various moral dilemmas.

What are moral dilemmas?

- ✓ Moral dilemmas are situations in which two or more moral obligations, duties, rights, goods, or ideals come into conflict with each other.
- ✓ The crucial feature of a moral dilemma is that all the moral principles cannot be fully respected in a given situation.
- ✓ Also solving one moral principle can create two or more conflicting applications for a particular situation.

Causes of Moral Dilemmas

Moral dilemmas are situations, mostly, due to the following three problems.

1. Problem of vagueness;

2. Problem of conflicting reasons; and
3. Problem of disagreement.

1. Problem of vagueness

- ✓ Vague means not clearly expressed or perceived; not specific or exact.
- ✓ For a given situation, sometimes it is unclear to the engineers to apply the most appropriate moral considerations or principles. They may not know how and which moral principles to be used in resolving a moral problem. This situation creates a typical moral dilemma.
- ✓ Example: consider an engineer, starting a new assignment as quality inspector checking the incoming raw materials/spare parts from the suppliers. Supplier offers (on behalf of some festival, say, Deepavali) him an expensive DVD player as a gift.

Now this situation is a moral dilemma. Because the engineer is unclear about: what to do? whether to accept the gift or not? whether the thing offered is a gift or a bribe? will it create a conflict of interest? Thus, the problem of vagueness i.e., unclarity causes a moral dilemma.

2. Problem of conflicting reasons

a. This is a situation where two or more moral problems conflicting each other, each of which seems to be correct.
b. In other words, this is a situation where two or more moral obligations, duties, rights or ideals come into conflict with each other; independently each one is good and correct. But when they come together it is very difficult choice to choose the good one. This situation is another moral dilemma.
c. Example: let us examine the space shuttle challenger explosion, focusing on the dilemma faced by the engineering manager, bob Lund. He had the following conflicts:

    a. Launching the challenger space shuttle despite there was an unknown probability that the shuttle would explode; which will kill all the persons on the board.
    b. Postponing the launch, which may lead to loss of future contracts from NASA, the loss of job to many workers, etc.

Now, the job of Bob Lund is to make the best choice out of the set conflicts. At last, he chose to risk the launching of shuttle. This situation is one of the good illustrations for the moral dilemma due to the problem of conflicting reasons.

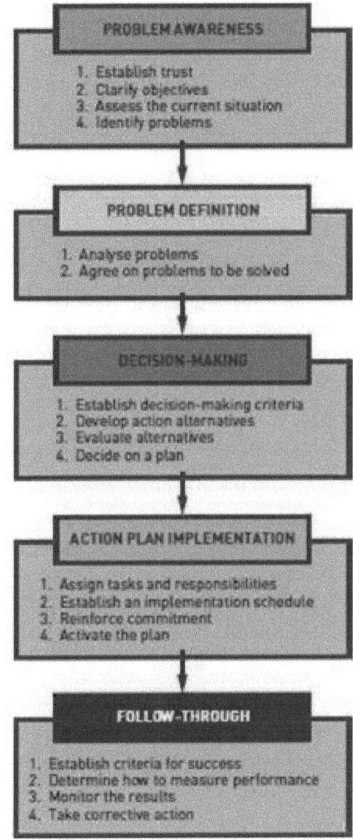

3. Problem of disagreement

a. It is quite obvious that individuals and groups may have different views, suggestions, interpretations, and solutions on a moral problem in particular situations. This disagreement among individuals and groups on interpreting moral issues will create a situation of another moral dilemma.
b. Example: In most corporations, there are disagreements among managers regarding whether customer can be allowed to inspect their plants and procedures, as a confidence building measure.

1.4 MORAL AUTONOMY

- This is viewed as the skill and habit of thinking rationally about ethical issues on the basis of moral concerns independently or by self-determination.
- Autonomous individuals think for themselves and do not assume that customs are always right.
- They seek to reason and live by general principles.
- Their motivation is to do what is morally reasonable for its own sake, maintaining integrity, self-respect, and respect for others.

"One who breaks an unjust law must do so openly, lovingly, and with a willingness to accept the penalty. I submit that an individual who breaks a law that conscience tells him is unjust and willingly accepts the penalty…is in reality expressing the highest respect for the law." *Rev. Martin Luther King, Jr.* in Letter from a Birmingham Jail,1963.

What is meant by moral autonomy?

- ✓ As already discussed, the practical aim in studying and teaching this engineering ethics course is to foster the moral autonomy of future engineers.
- ✓ Autonomy means self-determining 'or independent '.
- ✓ Moral autonomy is the ability to think critically and independently about moral issues and apply this normal thinking to situations that arise during the professional engineering practice.
- ✓ In other words, moral autonomy means the skill and habit of thinking rationally on ethical issues based on moral concern.
- ✓ That is, it is concerned with the independent attitude of an individual related to ethical issues.
- ✓ It is the ability to arrive at reasoned moral views based on the responsiveness to human values.

A person becomes morally autonomous by improving various practical skills listed below:

a. Proficiency is recognizing moral problems and issues in engineering.
b. Skill in comprehending, clarifying and critically assessing arguments on opposing sides of moral issues.
c. The ability to form consistent and comprehensive viewpoints based upon consideration of relevant facts.
d. Awareness of alternate responses to issues and creative solutions for practical difficulties.
e. Sensitivity to genuine difficulties and subtleties
f. Increased precision in the use of a common ethical language necessary to express and also defend one's views adequately.
g. Appreciation of possibilities of using rational dialogue in resolving moral conflicts and the need for tolerance of differences in perspective among orally reasonable people.
h. A sense of importance of integrating one's professional life and personal convictions i.e. maintaining one's moral integrity.

1.6 KHOLBERG VIEWS

Kohlberg Theory: These theories are based on the sorts of reasoning and motivation adopted by individuals with regard to moral questions.

Lawrence Kohlberg's Theory

- ✓ According to Kohlberg, the people progressed in their moral reasoning through a series of stages. His theory is based on the foundation that morality is a form of reasoning that develops I structural stages.
- ✓ The three levels of moral development, suggested by Kohlberg, are:
  1. Pre-conventional level;
  2. Conventional level; and
  3. Post –conventional level.

1. **Pre- conventional level**
   - ✓ The pre-conventional level of moral development is based to derive benefits for oneself.
   - ✓ In the first level, individual behave according to socially acceptable norms, which are taught mainly by parents and teachers.
   - ✓ At this level, individuals are motivated mainly by their interest to avoid punishment, or by their desire to satisfy their own needs, or by the external power exerted on them.
   - ✓ This is the level of development of all young children and some adults, who are unable to reach beyond a certain limit.

2. **Conventional level**
   - ✓ In the second level, the moral thinking and behavior of the individual are determined by the standards of their family, community, and society. That is, the norms or customs of one 's family/community/society are accepted and adopted as the ultimate standard of morality.
   - ✓ At this level, individuals are motivated by the desire to please others and to meet the social units 'expectations, without bothering much about their self-interest.
   - ✓ Thus, asper these Cond level, individuals give more importance to loyalty and close identification with others, than their own self-interest.
   - ✓ Many studies of Kohlberg reveal that most adults are living at this level only.
   - ✓ The second level of moral thinking is found in society generally. That's why it is named as _conventional 'level of moral development

3. **Post –Conventional level**
   - ✓ In the post-conventional level, the individuals are guided by strong principles and convictions, not by selfish needs or pressures from society.
   - ✓ According to Kohlberg, these individuals are called as autonomous ', because they think for/by themselves and also they do not believe that customs are always right.
   - ✓ The people at this level want to live by general principles that are universally applied to all people. They always desire to maintain their moral integrity, self-Kohlberg felt that the majority of adults do not reach the post-conventional level.

<table>
<tr><td colspan="3" align="center">Kohlberg Stages of Moral Development</td></tr>
<tr><td align="center">Approximate Age Range</td><td align="center">Stage</td><td align="center">Substages</td></tr>
<tr><td align="center">Birth to 9</td><td align="center">Preconventional</td><td>1) Avoid punishment
2) Gain Reward</td></tr>
<tr><td align="center">Age 9 to 20</td><td align="center">Conventional</td><td>3) Gain Approval & Avoid Disapproval
4) Duty & Guilt</td></tr>
<tr><td align="center">Age 20+ maybe never</td><td align="center">Postconventional</td><td>5) Agreed upon rights
6) Personal moral standards</td></tr>
</table>

1.7 GILLIGAN VIEWS

Gilligan Theory
- ✓ Carol Gilligan, a former student and colleague of Kohlberg, has criticized Kohlberg 's theory as male lased.
- ✓ She also charged Kohlberg that Kohlberg 's studies were concluded with male samples only and also his approach is dominated by a typical preoccupation with general rules and rights.
- ✓ According to Gilligan, males have tendency to over-ride the importance of moral rules and convictions while resolving moral dilemmas; whereas females have tendency to try hard to preserve personal relationships with all people involved in a situation.
- ✓ Also, Gilligan felt that men mostly focus their attention on content of the problem, whereas women focus their attention on the context i.e., situation of the problem.
- ✓ Gilligan refresher context-oriented emphasis on maintaining personal relationships as the ethics of care, and contrasts it with Kohlberg 's ethics of rules and right.

Gilligan's Levels of Moral Development

1. **Pre-conventional level**
   - ✓ This is almost the same as Kohlberg 's first level.
   - ✓ That is, in this level an individual is concerned with self-centered reasoning.
2. **Conventional level**
   - ✓ According to Gilligan, women will not hurt others and have a willingness to sacrifice their own interests in order to help others.
   - ✓ This level differs from Kohlberg 's second level.
3. **Post-conventional level**
   - ✓ This level also differs from Kohlberg 's third level.
   - ✓ In this level, the individual is able to maintain balance between his own needs with the needs of others. The balancing can be achieved through of importance.

Gilligan's Stages of the Ethic of Care		
Approximate Age Range	**Stage**	**Goal**
not listed	Preconventional	Goal is individual survival
Transition is from selfishness -- to -- responsibility to others		
not listed	Conventional	Self sacrifice is goodness
Transition is from goodness -- to -- truth that she is a person too		
maybe never	Postconventional	Principle of nonviolence: do not hurt others or self

Differences between the TWO THEORIES

KOHLBERG	GILLIGAN
Ethics of rules and rights	*Ethics of care*
Studies based on well educated, white male's only, tending male bias.	*Studies included females and colored peoples*
Application of abstract rules ranked in the order of importance	*Application of context-oriented reasoning.*
Studies were hypothesized for both the genders even though the study was conducted mostly on males	*Study was conducted on both genders and it was found, men based their reasoning on 'justice' and women based theirs on 'care'*

HEINZ'S DILEMMA

The famous example used by Kohlberg was called "Heinz's dilemma". A woman living in Europe would die of cancer unless she was given an expensive drug. Her husband, Heinz, could not afford it. But the local pharmacist, who had invented the drug at only one tenth of the sale price refused to sell it to Heinz who could only raise half the required money from borrowings. Desperation drives Heinz to break into the pharmacy and steal the drug to save his wife. When respondents were asked whether and why Heinz should or should not steal a drug to save his wife from a life-threatening illness. The responses of the individuals were compared with a prototypical response of individuals at particular stages of moral reasoning. Kohlberg noted that irrespective of the level of the individual the response could be same, but the reasoning could be different. For example, if a child reasoning at a 'preconvention' level might say that it is not right to steal because it is against law and someone might see you. At a 'conventional' level, an individual might argue that it is not right to steal because it is against law and laws are necessary for society to function. At a 'post conventional' level, one may argue that stealing is wrong because is against law and it is immoral.

ACT AND RULES UTILITARIAN

Theory of human rights ethics

- ✓ The rights ethicists emphasize that any action that violates any moral right is considered as ethically unacceptable.
- ✓ This theory holds that those actions are good that respect the rights of the individual.
- ✓ In other words, rights ethics holds that people have fundamental rights that other people have a duty to respect.
- ✓ Two versions of right ethics are:
    1. Locke 's version of rights ethics, and
    2. Meldon 's version of right ethics

Locke's version of rights ethics

- ✓ John locke (163-1704) a famous rights ethicist, argued that humans have human rights to life, liberty, and the property generated by one's labor.
- ✓ His views human rights either were considered as highly individualistic.
- ✓ In Locke's view, rights are claims that prevent other people from interfering in one 's life. These rights are referred as _liberty rights 'or _negative rights 'that place duties on other people not to interfere with one's life.

Malden's version of rights ethics

- ✓ Melden (1910-1991) considered human rights as intimately related to communities of people.
- ✓ According to Melden, moral rights require the capacity to show concern for other and to be accountable within a moral community.
- ✓ Melden also defined welfare rights as rights to community benefits needed living a minimum decent human life.

Similarities between duty ethics and rights ethics

- ✓ In fact, duty ethics and right ethics are like two different sides of the same coin.
- ✓ Both the theories focus and achieve the same end result. The end result is that individual persons must be respected, and actions are ethical that maintain this respect for the individual.
- ✓ As per duty ethics, people have duties, a primary one of which is to protect the rights of others
- ✓ But according to right ethics, people have fundamental rights that others have duties to protect

Difficulties in implementing duty and rights ethics theories

The two principal difficulties with the duty and rights ethics theories are:

- ✓ It is sometimes very difficult to prioritize the rights of individuals or groups. Because the basic rights of an individual or groups of individuals may conflict with the basic rights of another group.

✓ Since both the theories concern more about the good of an individual, therefore sometimes the overall good of society is not given much importance.

Tests for evaluating ethical theories
✓ Theory must be clear and logical. The concepts of theory should be formulated to enhance applicability.
✓ The theory should be consistent with its principles. The principles of the same theory should not contradict each other.
✓ The theory and its defense should rely only upon facts, truths, and correct information.
✓ The theory should be adequately complete so that to provide guidance for our required specific situations.
✓ The theory should be well- matched with moral convictions such as judgments, and intuitions about concrete situations.

What is meant by utility?
Utility can be defined as an overall balance between good and bad consequences of an action, taking into account the consequences for everyone affected.

Rule utilitarianism
✓ Rule utilitarianism differs from act utilitarianism in owning that moral rules are more important than an individual 'section.
✓ Richard Brandt proposed this version of utilitarianism.
✓ According to Brandt, though sticking to general moral rules such as don 't lies, don 't steal, be honest, don 't harm others, etc might not always maximize good in a particular situation, overall, sticking to moral rules will ultimately guide to the best.

Act utilitarianism
✓ The act utilitarianism concept was developed by John Stuart Mill (180-1873).
✓ The act utilitarianism focuses on individual actions rather than on general rules.
✓ It is understood that most of the common rules of morality such s don't lie, don't steal, be honest, don't harm others, keep promises etc are good guidelines to judge a human begin. But according to Mill, a person's actions should be judged based on whether the greatest good was achieved in a given situation. He also emphasized that even the general rules should be broken, if necessary, to achieve the greatest good for the greatest number of people.
✓ Mill's view about "goodness"
✓ As we know, the standard of right action is maximizing goodness, according to Mill, the term goodness represents two things.
✓ Intrinsic good: intrinsic good is something good in and of itself, or desirable for its own sake. He felt that happiness is the only intrinsic good.
✓ Instrumental goods: instrumental goods are other good things that provide means for happiness.

✓ In Mill's view, the pleasures derived through intellectual inquiry, creative accomplishment, appreciation of beauty, friendship, and love are inherently better than the bodily pleasures derived from eating, sex, and exercise

1.8 CONSENSUS AND CONTROVERSY

CONTROVERSY:
- All individuals will not arrive at same verdict during their exercising their moral autonomy.
- Aristotle noted long ago that morality is not as precise and clear-cut as arithmetic.
- Aim of teaching engineering ethics is not to get unanimous conformity of outlook by indoctrination, authoritarian and dogmatic teaching, hypnotism or any other technique but to improve promotion of tolerance in the exercise of moral autonomy.

CONSENSUS: The conductor of a music orchestra has authority over the musicians and his authority is respected by them by consensus as otherwise the music performance will suffer. Hence the authority and autonomy are compatible.

On the other hand, tension arises between the needs for autonomy and the need for concerns about authority. The difference between the two should be discussed openly to resolve the issue to the common good

Models of professional roles (Professional roles to be played by an engineer)
It is understood that an engineer has to play many roles while exercising his professional obligations. Some of the professional roles or models are given below:
1. **Engineers as Saviors**
    ✓ It is believed that engineers hold the key for any improvements in society through technological developments.
    ✓ Thus, some people consider engineer as a savior because they redeem society from poverty, inefficiency, waste and the hardships drudgery of manual labor.
2. **Engineers as Guardians**
    ✓ Engineersknowthedirectioninwhichtechnologyshoulddevelopandthespeedat which it should move. Thus, many people agree the role of engineers as guardians, as engineers guard the best interests of society.
3. **Engineers as Bureaucratic Servants**
    ✓ The engineers 'role in the management is to be the servant who receives and translates the directives of management into solid accomplishments.
    ✓ Thus, the engineers act as a bureaucratic servant i.e., loyal organizations set by the management.
4. **Engineers as Social Servants**
    a. As we know, engineers have to play the role of social servants to receive society 's directives and to satisfy society 's desires
5. **Engineers as Social Enablers and Catalysts**

a. Besides merely practicing the management 's directives, the engineers have to play a role of creating a better society. Also they should act as catalysts for making social changes.

b. Sometimes engineers have to help the management and the society to understand their needs and to make decisions about desirable technological development.

6. **Engineers as Game Players**

a. In actual practice, engineers are neither servant nor master so for anyone. In fact, they play the economic game rules, which may be effective at a given time.

b. Like managers, the engineers 'aim is also to play successfully within the organization and moving ahead in a competitive world

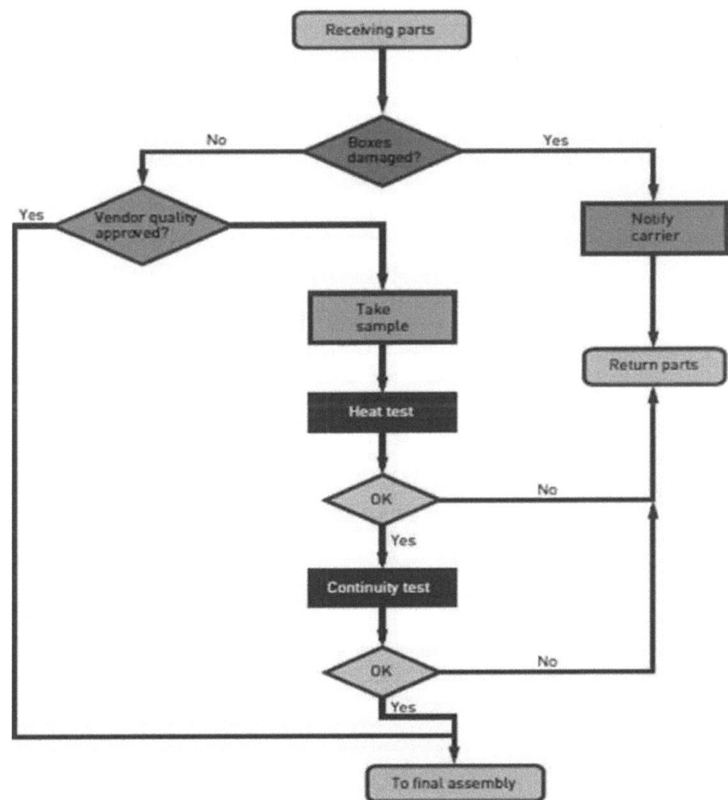

Consensus and Controversy

- ✓ Literally, consensus means agreement ', and controversy means disagreement '.
- ✓ When an individual exercise moral autonomy, he may not be able to attain the same results as other people obtain in practicing their moral autonomy. Here there might be some differences in the practical application of moral autonomy. This kind of controversies i.e., disagreements are inevitable.
- ✓ Since exercising moral autonomy is not as precise and clear-cut as arithmetic, therefore the moral disagreements are natural and common. So in order to allow scope for disagreement, the tolerance is required among individuals with autonomous, reasonable and responsible thinking.
- ✓ According to the principle of tolerance, the objective of teaching and studying engineering ethics is to discover ways of promoting tolerance in the exercise of moral autonomy by engineers.
- ✓ Thus, the goal of teaching engineering ethics is not merely producing always a unanimous moral conformity; it is about finding the proper ways and means for promoting tolerance in the practical applications of moral autonomy by engineers.
- ✓ In a way, the goal of courses on engineering ethics and goals of responsible engineering have some similarities. Both situations require the need for some consensus regarding the role of authority.
- ✓ Relationship between autonomy and authority
    1. Moral autonomy and respect for authority are compatible with each other. Exercising moral autonomy is based on the moral concern for other people and recognition of good moral reasons. Also, moral autonomy emphasizes the capabilities and responsibilities of people. Authority provides the framework through which learning attitudes are encouraged.
    2. Sometimes, conflicts will arise between individuals 'need for autonomy and the need for consensus about authority. This situation can be rescued by having open and frank discussion regarding a moral issue with the help of authority.
- ✓ Illustration: Consider the relationship between autonomy and authority, with reference to a classroom. In the classroom, the teachers have authority over students. Authority of the teachers helps in maintaining the dignity and decorum of academic climate in a institution; also in restoring the confidence and respect between teachers and students.

As per the first point, there should be the acceptance of authority of authority by both the teachers and students, in order to conduct the classes in orderly ways. When the authority is misused, conflicts may arise between autonomy and authority. As per the second point, allowing open discussions between teachers and students can reduce the unhealthy academic atmosphere.

1.9 PROFESSION AND PROFESSIONALISM

Engineers normally imagine that they are servants to organizations rather than a public guardian. Responsibility to the public is essential for a professional.

Who is a professional? Obviously, a *member* of a profession.

What is a profession? 'JOB' or 'OCCUPATION' that meets the following criteria from which a person *earns his living.*

- Knowledge – Exercise of skills, knowledge, judgment and discretion requiring extensive formal criteria.
- Organization - special bodies by members of the profession to set standard codes of ethics,
- Public good-The occupation serves some important public good indicated by a code of ethics.

Who is a professional engineer?

- Has a bachelor's degree in engineering from an accredited school
- Performs engineering work
- Is a registered and licensed Professional Engineer
- Acts in a morally responsible way while practicing engineering Differing views on Professionals

"Only consulting engineers who are basically independent and have freedom from coercion can be called as professionals."   -Robert L Whitelaw

"Professionals have to meet the expectations of clients and employers. Professional restraints are to be imposed by only laws and government regulations and not by personal conscience."
-Samuel Florman

"Engineers are professionals when they 1) attain standards of achievement in education, job performance or creativity in engineering and 2) accept the most basic moral responsibilities to the public as well as employers, clients, colleagues and subordinates."   -Mike Martin & Rol and Schinzinger

MOTIVES FOR PROFESSIONALISM

- A desire for interesting and challenging work and the pleasure in the act of changing the world.
- The joy of creative efforts. Where a scientist's interest is in discovering new technology, engineers' interest is derived from creatively solving practical problems.
- The engineer shares the scientist's job in understanding the laws and riddles of the universe.

- The sheer magnitude of the nature–oceans, rivers, mountains and prairies–leads engineers to build engineering marvels like ships, bridges, tunnels, etc., which appeal to human passion.
- The pleasure of being in the presence of machines generating a comforting and absorbing sense of a manageable, controlled and ordered world.
- Strong sense of helping, of directing efforts towards easing the lot of one's fellows.

The main pleasure of the engineer will always be to contribute to the well-being of his fellow-men.

MODELS OF PROFESSIONAL ROLES

Promotion of public good is the primary concern of the professional engineers. There are several role models to whom the engineers are attracted. These models provoke their thinking, attitudes and actions.

1. **Savior:** The engineer as a savior, save the society from poverty, illiteracy, wastage, inefficiency, ill health, human (labor) dignity and lead it to prosperity, through technological development and social planning. For example, R.L. Stevenson.
2. **Guardian:** He guards the interests of the poor and general public. As one who is conversant with technology development, is given the authority befitting his expertise to determine what is best suited to the society. For example, Lawrence of Arabia (an engineer).
3. **Bureaucratic Servant:** He serves the organization and the employers. The management of an enterprise fixes its goals and assigns the job of problem solving to the engineer, who accepts the challenge and shapes the min to concrete achievements. For example, Jamshedji Tata.
4. **Social Servant:** It is one who exhibits social responsibility. The engineer translates the interest and aspirations of the society into a reality, remembering that his true master is the society at large. For example, Sir M. Viswesvarayya.
5. **Social Enabler and Catalyst:** One who changes the society through technology. The engineer must assist the management and the society to understand their needs and make informed decisions on the desirable technological development and minimize the negative effects of technology on people and their living environment. Thus, he shines as a social enabler and a catalyst for further growth. For example, Sri Sundarlal Bahuguna.
6. **Game Player:** He is neither a servant nor master. An engineer is an assertive player, not a passive player who may carry out his master 's voice. He plays a unique role successfully within the organization, enjoying the excitement of the profession and having the satisfaction of surging ahead in a competitive world. For example, Narayanamurthy, Infosys and Dr. Kasthurirangan, ISRO.

1.10   VIRTUE ETHICS

- *"The unexamined life is not worth living."*

(Socrates, 470-399 B.C.)

- *"The happy life is thought to be virtuous; now a virtuous life requires exertion and does not consist in amusement."*   (Aristotle, 384-322B.C.)

The Four Main Virtues

- Prudence (mind): to think about a moral problem clearly and completely
- Temperance (emotions): control attraction to positive emotions
- Fortitude (emotions): control aversion for negative emotions
- Justice (will): choose according to truth and fairness.

Virtue Ethics

- Focuses on the type of person we should strive to be
- Actions which reflect *good character* traits (virtues) are inherently *right*
- Actions which reflect *bad character* traits (vices) are inherently *wrong*
- Virtue ethics are tied more to individual behavior than to that of an organization (e.g., business, government)

ARISTOTLE; says that moral virtues are tendencies, acquired through habit formation, to reach a proper balance between extremes in conduct, emotion, desire and attitude i.e., virtues are tendencies to find the Golden Mean between the extremes of too much and too little.

Some of the virtues are defined using examples here:

Virtue	Too much	Too less
(Golden mean between extremes)		
Courage	*Foolhardiness*	*Cowardice*
Truthfulness	*Revealing all in violation of tact and confidentiality*	*Being secretive or lacking in candor*
Generosity	*Wasting one's resources*	*Being miserly*
Friendliness	*Being annoyingly effusive*	*Sulky or surly*

PROFESSIONAL RESPONSIBILITY

- Being morally responsible as a professional.
- Most basic and comprehensive professional virtue.
- Creation of useful and safe technological products while respecting the autonomy of clients and public, especially in matters of risk taking.

This encompasses a wide variety of the more specific virtues grouped as follows:

a. SELF DIRECTIONVIRTUES: Fundamental virtues in exercising our moral autonomy and responsibility. e.g., self-understanding, humility, good moral judgment, courage, self-discipline, perseverance, commitments, self-respect and dignity

b. PUBLIC SPIRITED VIRTUES: Focusing on the good of the clients and public affected by the engineers' work by not directly and intentionally harming others i.e. 'nonmaleficence'. Beneficence, sense of community, generosity are other virtues falling in this category.

c. TEAMWORKVIRTUES: Enables professionals to work successfully with others. E.g., collegiality, cooperativeness, the ability to communicate, respect for authority, loyalty to employers and leadership qualities.

d. PROFICIENCYVIRTUES: Mastery of one's craft that characterize good engineering practice e.g., competence, diligence, creativity, self-renewal through continuous education.

MORAL INTEGRITY

Moral integrity is the unity of character on the basis of moral concern, and especially on the basis of honesty. The unity is consistency among our attitudes, emotions and conduct in relation to justified moral values.

SELF-RESPECT

- Valuing oneself in morally appropriate ways.
- Integral to finding meaning in one's life and work
- A pre-requisite for pursuing other moral ideals and virtues.
- Self-respect is a moral concept of properly valuing oneself but self-esteem is a psychological concept of positive attitude towards one self.

Self-respect takes two forms.

1. *Recognition self-respect* is properly valuing oneself because of one's inherent moral worth, the same worth that every other human being has.
2. *Appraisal self-respect* is properly valuing ourselves according to how well we meet

1.11   ETHICAL THEORIES

Independently propounded ethical theories are many and are very diverse in nature.
Philosophical point of view of ethical theories
Deontology: Deontological ethics or deontology (from Greek δέον, deon, "obligation, duty"; and - λογία, -logia) is an approach to ethics that determines goodness or rightness from examining acts, or the rules and duties that the person doing the act strove to fulfill. This is in contrast to consequentialism, in which rightness is based on the consequences of an act, and not the act by itself. In deontology, an act may be considered right even if the act produces a bad consequence,

if it follows the rule that "one should do unto others as they would have done unto them", and even if the person who does the act lacks virtue and had a bad intention in doing the act. According to deontology, we have a duty to act in a way that does those things that are inherently good as acts ("truth-telling" for example), or follow an objectively obligatory rule (as in rule utilitarianism). For deontologists, the ends or consequences of our actions are not important in and of themselves, and our intentions are not important in and of themselves. Immanuel Kant's theory of ethics is considered deontological for several different reasons. First, Kantar guest hat to act in the morally right way, people must act from duty(deon). Second, Kant argued that it was not the consequences of actions that make them right or wrong but the motives (maxime) of the person who carries out the action. Kant's argument that to act in the morally right way, one must act from duty, begins with an argument that the highest good must be both good in itself, and good without qualification. Something is 'good in itself' when it is intrinsically good, and 'good without qualification' when the addition of that thing never makes a situation ethically worse. Kant then argues that those things that are usually thought to be good, such as intelligence, perseverance and pleasure, fail to be either intrinsically good or good without qualification. Pleasure, for example, appears to not be good without qualification, because when people take pleasure in watching someone suffering, this seems to make the situation ethically worse. He concludes that there is only one thing that is truly good: Nothing in the world—indeed nothing even beyond the world—can possibly be conceived which could be called good without qualification except a good will.

Kantian ethics: Kantian ethics are deontological, revolving entirely around duty rather than emotions or end goals. All actions are performed in accordance with some underlying maxim or principle, which are deeply different from each other; it is according to this that the moral worth of any action is judged. Kant's ethics are founded on his view of rationality as the ultimate good and his belief. that all people are fundamentally rational beings. This led to the most important part of Kant's ethics, the formulation of the categorical imperative, which is the criterion for whether a maxim is good or bad. Simply, put, this criterion amount to a thought experiment: to attempt to universalize the maxim (by imagining a world where all people necessarily acted in this way in the relevant circumstances) and then see if the maxim and its associated action would still be conceivable in such a world. For instance, holding the maxim kill anyone who annoys you and applying it universally would result in a world which would soon bed avoid of people and without anyone left to kill. Thus, holding this maxim is irrational as it ends up being impossible to hold it. Universalizing a maxim (statement) leads to it being valid, or to one of two contradictions — a contradiction in conception (where the maxim, when universalized, is no longer viable means to the end) or a contradiction in will (where the will of a person contradicts what the universalization of the maxim implies).

The first type leads to a "perfect duty", and these Cond leads to an "imperfect duty. "Kant's ethics focus then only on the maxim that underlies actions and judges these to be good or bad solely on how they conform to reason. Kant showed that many of our common-sense views of what is good or bad conform to his system but denied that any action performed for reasons other than rational actions can be good (saving some on who is drowning simply out of a great pity for them is not a morally good act). Kant also denied that the consequences of an act in any way contribute to the moral worth of that act, his reasoning being (highly simplified for brevity) that the physical world is outside our full control and thus we cannot be held accountable for the events that occur in it.

Virtue ethics: Virtue ethics describes the character of a moral agent as a driving force for ethical behavior, and is used to describe the ethics of Socrates, Aristotle, and other early Greek philosophers. Socrates (469 BC – 399 BC) was one of the first Greek philosophers to encourage both scholars and the common citizen to turn their attention from the outside world to the condition of humankind. In this view, knowledge having a bearing on human life was placed highest, all other knowledge being secondary. Self-knowledge was considered necessary for success and inherently an essential good. A self-aware person will act completely within his capabilities to his pinnacle, while an ignorant person will flounder and encounter difficulty. To Socrates, a person must become aware of every fact (and its context) relevant to his existence, if he wishes to attain self-knowledge. He posited that people will naturally do what is good, if they know what is right. Evil or bad actions are the result of ignorance. If a criminal was truly aware of the mental and spiritual consequences of his actions, he would neither commit nor even consider committing those actions. Any person who knows what is truly right will automatically do it, according to Socrates. While he correlated knowledge with virtue, he similarly equated virtue with happiness. The truly wise man will know what is right, do what is good, and therefore be happy.

	Consequentialism	Deontology	Virtue Theory
example	Mill's utilitarianism	Kantian ethics	Aristotle's moral theory
abstract description	An action is right if it promotes the best consequences.	An action is right if it is in accordance with a moral rule or principle.	An action is right if it is what a virtuous agent would do in the circumstances.
more concrete specification	The best consequences are those in which happiness is maximized.	A moral rule is one that is required by rationality.	A virtuous agent is one who acts virtuously, that is, one who has and exercises the virtues. A virtue is a character trait a human being needs to flourish or live well.

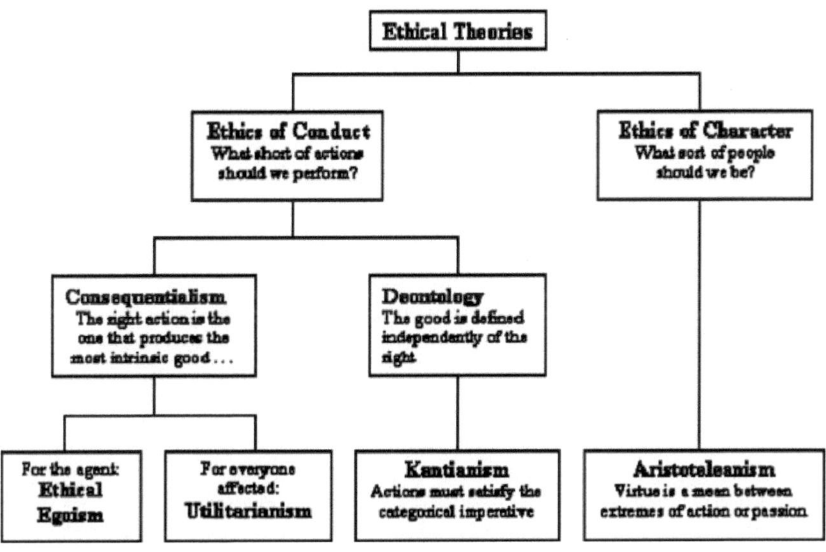

Philosophers have found ethical theories useful because they help us decide why various actions are right and wrong. If it is generally wrong to punch someone then it is wrong to kick them for the same reason. We can then generalize that it is wrong to —h arm ‖people to help understand why punching and kicking tend to both be wrong, which helps us decide whether or not various other actions and institutions are wrong, such as capital punishment, abortion, homosexuality, atheism, and so forth. All of the ethical theories have various strengths and it is possible that more than one of them is true (or at least accurate). Not all moral theories are necessarily incompatible. Imagine that utilitarianism, the categorical imperative, and Stoic virtue ethics are all true. In that case true evaluative beliefs (e.g. human life is preferable) would tell us which values to promote (e.g. human life), and we would be more likely to have an emotional response that would motivate us to actually promote the value. We would feel more satisfied about human life being promoted (e.g. through a cure to cancer) and dissatisfied about human life being destroyed (e.g. through war). Finally, what is right for one person would be right for everyone else in a sufficiently similar situation because the same reasons will justify the same actions.

TYPES OF ETHICAL THEORIES

S.NO	TYPES	BASED ON
1	Virtue ethics	Virtues and vices
2	Utilitarianism	best for most people
3	Duty ethics	Duties to respect persons
4	Rights ethics	Human Rights

CIVIC VIRTUE

Civic virtue is the moral under pinning of how a citizen behaves and is involved in society. It is a standard of righteous behavior in relation to a citizens' involvement in society. A individual may exhibit civic virtue by voting, volunteering and organizing other community activities. Without an understanding of civic virtue, citizens are less likely to look beyond their families, friends and economic interests. They are less likely to help others in the community, to volunteer their time, to give to nonprofit organizations or to participate in group activity that benefits society. Related ideas for civic virtue are citizenship, philanthropy, public good, voluntarism and social capital

HUMAN VALUES

The Story of a Carpenter

An elderly carpenter was ready to retire. He told his employer-contractor of his plans to leave the house- building business and live a more leisurely life with his wife enjoying his extended family.

He would miss his paycheck, but he needed to retire. They could get by. The contractor was sorry to see his good worker go and asked if he could build just one more house as a personal favor.

The carpenter said yes, but in time it was easy to see that his heart was not in his work. He resorted to shoddy workmanship and used inferior materials. It was an unfortunate way to end his career.

When the carpenter finished his work and the builder came to inspect the house, the contractor handed over the house key to the carpenter. "This is your house," he said, "it is my parting gift to you."

What a shock! What a Shame! If only he had known he was building his own house, he would have done it all so differently. Now he had to live in the home he built none too well.

(Modified from LIVING WITH HONOUR by SHIV KHERA) Do we find ourselves in similar situations as the carpenter?

Moving through our work hours fast paced, driven to "get the job done", without much thought to moral values.

How do we regain our focus as individuals and organizations? This is the challenge for the employee and the employer. Ethics are fundamental standards of conduct by which we work as a professional

VALUES
- ➢ Values are individual in nature.
- ➢ Values are comprised of personal concepts of responsibility, entitlement and respect.
- ➢ Values are shaped by personal experience, may change over the span of a lifetime and may be influenced by lessons learned.
- ➢ Values may vary according to an individual's cultural, ethnic and/or faith- based background.

"Never change your core values."

In spite of all the change around you, decide upon what you will never change: your core values. Take your time to decide what they are but once you do, do not compromise on them for any reason. Integrity is one such value.

MORALS
- ➢ Morals are guiding principles that every citizen should hold.
- ➢ Morals are foundational concepts defined on both an individual and societal level.
- ➢ At the most basic level, morals are the knowledge of the difference between right and wrong.

PERSONAL ETHICS
- *a.* Simply put, all individuals are morally autonomous beings with the power and right to choose their values, but it does not follow that all choices and all value systems have an equal claim to be called ethical.
- *b.* Actions and beliefs inconsistent with the Six Pillars of Character - trustworthiness, respect, responsibility, fairness, caring and citizenship - are simply not ethical.

PERSONAL ETHICS - everyday examples

a. Software piracy
b. Expense account padding
c. Copying of homework or tests
d. Income taxes
e. "Borrowing" nuts and bolts, office supplies from employer
f. Copying of Videos or CD's
g. Plagiarism
h. Using the copy machine at work

RELIGION AND ETHICS

a. The "Golden Rule" is a basic tenet in almost all religions: Christian, Hindu, Jewish, Confucian, Buddhist, Muslim.
b. "Do unto others as you would have others do unto you."
c. "Treat others as you would like them to treat you" (Christian). "Hurt not others with that which pains you" (Buddhist)
d. "What is hateful to yourself do not do to your fellow men" (Judaism)
e. "No man is a true believer unless he desires for his brother that which he desires for himself" (Islam)

MORALITY AND ETHICS
a. Concerns the goodness of voluntary human conduct that affects the self or other living things
b. Morality (Latin mores) usually refers to any aspect of human action
c. Ethics (Greek ethos) commonly refers only to professional behavior
d. Ethics consist of the application of fundamental moral principles and reflect our dedication to fair treatment of each other, and of society as a whole.
e. An individual's own values can result in acceptance or rejection of society's ethical standards because even thoughtfully developed ethical rules can conflict with individual values.

ASPECTS OF ETHICS

There are two aspects to ethics:
a. The first involves the ability to discern right from wrong, good from evil and propriety from impropriety.
b. The second involves the commitment to do what is right, good and proper. Ethics entails action.

An ALGEBRA course will teach you ALGEBRA. A HISTORY course will teach you HISTORY.

A MANAGEMENT course will teach you principles of MANAGEMENT.

But, Will an *ETHICS* course teach you to be *ETHICAL*? Think

UNIT-2
ENGINEERING AS SOCIAL EXPERIMENTATION

To undertake a great work and especially a work of novel type means, carrying out an experiment. It means taking up a struggle with the forces of nature without the assurance of emerging as a victor after the first attack- Louis Marie Henri Navier (1785 - 1836) - *Founder of Structural Analysis.*

2.1 ENGINEERING AS EXPERIMENTATION

- Experimentation (Preliminary tests or Simulations) plays a vital role in the design of a product or process.
- In all stages of converting a new engineering concept into a design like,
  a. first rough-cut design,
  b. usage of different types of materials and processes,
  c. detailed design,
  d. further stages of work design and
  e. the finished product,

Experiments and tests are conducted to evaluate the product. Modifications are made based on the outcome of these experiments. The normal design process is thus iterative (modifications being made on the basis of feedback information acquired from the tests).

Even though various tests and experiments are conducted at various stages, the engineering project as a whole in its *totality* can be viewed as an *experiment.*

SIMILARITIES TO STANDARD EXPERIMENTS

1. Any project is carried out in partial ignorance due to
   - The uncertainties in the abstract model used for the design calculations,
   - The uncertainties in the precise characteristics of the materials purchased,
   - The uncertainties caused by variations in processing and fabrication of materials and
   - The uncertainties about the nature of stresses the finished product will encounter.
2. Indeed, Engineer's success lies in the *ability to accomplish tasks* with only a *partial knowledge* of scientific laws about nature and society.
3. The final outcome of engineering projects, like those of experiments, is generally uncertain. Very often, possible outcomes are not even known and great risks may be presented which could never be thought of.
4. Effective Engineering relies upon knowledge gained about products both before and after they leave the factory- knowledge needed for improving current products and creating better ones. That is, ongoing success in engineering depends upon gaining new knowledge.

LEARNING FROM THE PAST

Engineers should learn not only from their own earlier design and operating results, but also from other engineers.

Engineers repeat the past mistakes of others due to the following reasons.

- Lack of established channels of communication.
- Misplaced pride in not asking for information
- Embarrassment at failure or fear of litigation (legal problems).
- Negligence.

Examples:

a. The *Titanic* lacked sufficient number of life boats resulting in the death of 1522 out of 2227(life boat capacity available was only 825), a few decades later *Arctic* per is due to the same problem.
b. In June 1966, a section of the Milford Haven Bridge in Wales collapsed during construction. A bridge of similar design, erected by the same bridge- builder in

Melbourne, Australia, also partially collapsed in the month of October, same year. During this incident 33 people were killed and many were injured.

    c. Malfunctions occurred at nuclear reactors at various locations and the information reports were with Babcock and Wilcox, there actor manufacturer. In spite of these, no attention was paid leading to a pressure relief valve giving rise to the Three Mile Island nuclear accident on March 28,1979.

CONTRASTS WITH STANDARD EXPERIMENTS

1. **EXPERIMENTAL CONTROL:** In standard experiments, members are in two different groups. Members of *one group receive special* experimental treatment. The other group members, called *'control group' do not receive* special treatment, though they are from the same environment in all other respects. But this is not true in engineering, since most of the experiments are not conducted in laboratories. The subjects of experiments are human beings who are outside the experimenter's control. Thus, it is not possible to study the effects of changes in variable on different groups. Hence only historical and retrospective data available about various target groups has to be used for evaluation. Hence engineering as a social experimentation seems to be an extended usage of the concept of experimentation.

2. **INFORMED CONSENT**: has two elements, *knowledge* and *voluntariness*. The subjects (human beings) should be given all the information needed to make a reasonable decision. Next, they must get into the experiment without being subjected to *force, fraud or deception*. Supplying complete information is neither necessary nor in most cases possible. But *all relevant information* needed for making are as on able decision on whether to participate should be conveyed. Generally, we all prefer to be the subject of our own experiments rather than those of somebody else.

Conditions defining *Informed or Valid Consent*

    a. The consent is given voluntarily

    b. The consent is based on information a rational person would want, together with any other information requested and presented to them in understandable form.

    c. The consenter was competent to process the information and make rational decisions.

    d. Information has been widely disseminated.

    e. The subject's consent is offered by proxy by a group that collectively represents many subjects like interests, concerns and exposure to risk.

'Engineering experiments are not conducted to gain new knowledge unlike scientific experiments. Is this distinction necessary? This distinction is not vital because we are concerned *about the manner* in which the experiment is conducted, such as *valid consent* of human subjects being sought, *safety measures* taken and means exist for *terminating* the experiment *at any time* and providing all participants a *safe exit*.

Features of morally responsible engineers in social experimentation

a. *Conscientiousness*: A primary obligation to protect the safety of human subjects and respect their right of consent.
b. *Relevant information*: A constant awareness of the experimental nature of any project, imaginative forecasting of its possible side effects and a reasonable effort to monitor them.
c. *Moral autonomy*: Autonomous, personal involvement in all steps of the project.
d. *Accountability*: Accepting accountability for the results of the project.

CONSCIENTIOUSNESS:

- ❖ Conscientious moral commitment means sensitivity to the full range of relevant moral values.
- ❖ Sensitivity to responsibilities that is relevant.
- ❖ Willingness to develop the skill and expend the effort needed to reach the best balance possible among these considerations.
- ❖ Conscientiousness means consciousness because mere intent is not sufficient.

Conceiving engineering as social experimentation restores the vision of engineers as guardians of the public interest in that they are duty bound to guard the welfare and safety of those affected by engg., projects.

RELEVANT INFORMATION:

Conscientiousness is blind without relevant factual information. Moral concern involves a commitment to obtain and assess all available pertinent information. Another dimension to factual information is the consequences of what one does. While regarding engg as social experimentation points out the importance of context, it also urges the engineer to view his or her specialized activities in a project as part of a larger whole having a social impact that may involve a variety of unintended effects. It may be better to practice 'defensive engg' (Chauncy Starr) or 'preventive engg' (Ruth Davis).

MORAL AUTONOMY

- ❖ People are morally autonomous when their moral conduct and principles of action are their own.
- ❖ Moral beliefs and attitudes must be a critical reflection and not a passive adoption of the particular conventions of one's society, religion or profession.
- ❖ Moral beliefs and attitudes cannot be agreed to formally and adhered to merely verbally.

- ❖ They must be integrated into the core of one's personality and should lead to committed action.
- ❖ It is wrong to think that as an employee when one performs '*acts*' serving company's interests, one is no longer morally and personally identified with one's actions.
- ❖ Viewing engg as a social experimentation helps to overcome this flawed thought and restores a sense of autonomous participation in one's work.
    a. As an experimenter, an engineer is exercising the specialized training that forms the core of one's identity as a professional
    b. A social experiment that can result in unknown consequences should help inspire a critical and questioning attitude about the adequacy of current and safety standards
    c. In turn, this leads to better personal involvement work

ACCOUNTABILITY

- ❖ Responsible people accept moral responsibility for their actions.
- ❖ Accountability is the willingness to submit one's actions to moral scrutiny and be open and responsive to the assessment of others.
- ❖ It should be understood as being culpable and blameworthy form is deeds.

Submission to an employer's authority creates in many people a narrow sense of accountability for the consequences of their action. This is because of

i) Only a small contribution is made by one individual, when large scale engineering work is fragmented. The final product which is far away from one's immediate work place, does not give a proper understanding of the consequences of one's action.

ii) Due to the fragmentation of work, a vast diffusion of accountability takes place. The area of personal accountability is delimited to the portion of work being carried out by one.

iii) The pressure to move on to another new project does not allow one to complete the observations long enough. This makes people accountable only for meeting schedules and not for the consequences of action.

iv) To avoid getting into legal issues, engineers tend to concentrate more on legal liabilities than the containment of the potential risks involved in their area of work.

Viewing engineering as a social experimentation makes one overcome these difficulties and see the problem in whole rather than as part.

2.2 ENGINEERS AS RESPONSIBLE EXPERIMENTS

General responsibility of engineering as society:

- Engineers are primarily considered as technical enablers or facilitators, rather than being the sole experimenters.
- Engineers 'responsibility is shared with management, the public and others.
- The other unique responsibility of engineers includes monitoring projects, identifying risks, providing customers and clients the required information to make reasonable decisions.
- While exercising engineering duties, the engineers should display the virtue of being morally responsible person.

General features of moral responsible engineers:
1. Conscientiousness
2. Relevant information
3. Moral Autonomy
4. Accountability

Conscientiousness
- Conscientiousness means commitment to live according to certain values. It implies conscientiousness.
- Engineers have to be sensitive to a range of moral values and responsibilities, which are relevant in a given situation.
- Also, engineers should have the willing to develop the skill and apply the effort needed to reach the best balance possible among various considerations.
- _Open eyes, open s and an open mind 'are required to evaluate a given situation, its implication and to determine who are involved or affected.
- The primary duty of morally responsible engineers is to protect the safety of human beings and respect their rights of consent.

Relevant information:
- Conscientiousness is impossible without relevant factual information.
- Engineers have to show the commitment to obtain and properly gauge all the information related to meeting one 's moral obligations.
- The two general ways of losing perspective on the   context of one's work are given below.
    1. To grasp the context of one's work, one should be aware of implication of that work.
    2. To shifts the responsibility and blames the others in the organization.

Thus, conceiving engineering as social experimentation, it is important that engineers act as **responsible agents.** The responsible agents require
- Imaginative forecasting of possible bad side effects
- The development of an attitude of _defensive engineering 'and _preventive technology '
- Careful monitoring of projects and

- Respect for people rights to give informed consent Moral autonomy;
- ✓ The moral autonomy is the ability to think critically and independently about moral issues and apply this moral thinking to situations that arise during the professional engineering practice.
- ✓ It is understood that an individual personality depends on the integration of his moral benefits and attitude.
- ✓ When one's labor and skills are sold, then it is an illusion to think that the person is not morally autonomous.
- ✓ As an experimenter, an engineer has to undergo an extensive and updated training to form his identity as a professional.
- ✓ There will be a personal involvement in one's work.
- ✓ The magnitude of moral autonomy to be experienced by engineering is highly influenced by the attitude of company 's managements.
- ✓ Where there is a treat for engineers 'moral autonomy, then engineers can look for moral support from their professional societies and outside organization.

Accountability:
- ✓ The term accountability 'means being responsible, liable, answerable or obligated.
- ✓ In proper terms, the accountability refers to the general tendency of being willing to submit ones action to any type of moral scrutiny and be responsive to others assessment.
- ✓ It involves a willingness to present morally convincing reason for ones action and conduct.
- ✓ Morally responsible people are expected to accept morally responsibility for their action.
- ✓ According to Stanely Milgram, people are not willing to accept personal accountability when placed under authority.
- ✓ There exist a lot of difference and separation between casual influence and moral accountability in all professions including engineering.
- ✓ Because of modern engineering practices, the complication in accepting one's moral accountability further worsened. Some of these situations are explained below:
  3. Modern engineering projects involve teamwork, in which each member contributes a small of personal accountability.
  4. The modern organization are based on the principle of _division of work'. Due to this division of work, the personal accountability also stretched within hierarchies of authority.

A preoccupation with legalities in a time of proliferating malpractice lawsuits. Even both the groups are subjected to same environment; the group that was not given the special treatment is called _**control group**".
- ✓ In engineering experiments, usually there is no control group. Sometimes the control group is used only when the project is limited to laboratory

experiments. Because the engineering experiments involve human beings are experimental subjects. In fact, clients and customers have more.

2.2 RESEARCH ETHICS

Andrew Oldenquist and Edward Slowter pointed out how the existence of separate codes for different professional societies can give members the feeling that ethical conduct is more relative than it is and that it can convey to the public the view that none is 'really right'. The current codes are by no means perfect but are definitely steps in the right direction.

The problems of law in engineering

1. The greatest problem of law in engg is of 'minimal compliance'. Engineers and employers can search for loopholes in the law to barely keep to its letter while violating its spirit. Engineers will tend to refer to standard readymade specifications rather than come up with innovative ideas. Minimal compliance led to the tragedy of the 'Titanic'.
2. Continually updating laws and regulations may be counter-productive and will make law always lag behind technology. This also overburdens the rules and regulators.
3. Many laws are 'non-laws' i.e. laws without enforce able sanctions. These merely serve as window dressing, frequently gives a false sense of security to the public.
4. The opponents of the law may burden it intentionally with many unreasonable provisions that are peal will not be far off.
5. Highly powerful organizations, like the government can violate the laws when they think they can get away with it by inviting would be challengers, to face the min lengthy and costly court proceedings. This also creates frustration with the law.

Role of law in engineering
1. It is wrong to write off rule-making and rule following as futile. Good laws, effectively enforced, clearly produce benefits.
2. Reasonable minimum standards are ensured of professional conduct.
3. It also provides a self-interested motive for most people and corporations to comply.
4. They also serve as powerful support and defense for those who wish to act ethically in situations where ethical conduct might not bewelcome.
5. Viewing engineering as social experimentation provides engineers with a better perspective on laws and regulations.
6. Precise rules and enforceable sanctions are appropriate in cases of ethical misconduct that involve violations of well-established and regularly re-examined procedures that have as their purpose the safety of public.

In areas of experimentation, rules must not attempt to cover all possible outcomes of an experiment, nor must they force the engineer to adopt a rigidly specified course of action. Here the regulations should be broad based guidelines but should hold the engineer accountable for his or her decisions.

2.3 CODE OF ETHICS

Introduction:
One of the trademarks of contemporary professions is code of ethics. Codes of ethics are propagated by various professional society. These codes of ethics are guidelines for specific group of professionalism to help them perform their roles; to know how to conduct themselves; and to know how to resolve around various ethical issues. These codes convey the rights, duties, and obligation of the members of the profession.

What is code of ethics?
- ✓ The primary aspects of codes of ethics are to provide the basic framework for ethical judgment for a professional.
- ✓ The codes of ethics are also referred to as the codes of conduct, express the commitment to ethical conduct shared by members of a profession.
- ✓ It expresses the ethical principles and standards in a coherent, comprehensive and accessible manner
- ✓ It also defines the role and responsibility of profession.
- ✓ It helps the professionals to apply moral and ethical principles to the specific situations encountered in professional practice.
- ✓ These codes are based on five canons i.e., principle of ethics-integrity, competence, individual responsibility, professional responsibility, and human concerns.
- ✓ It also be noted that ethical codes do not establish new ethical principles. They use only those principles that are already well established and widely accepted in society.
- ✓ Thus, the code of ethics creates an environment within a profession where ethical behavior is norm.

Positive Roles of Code of Ethics
The code of ethics propagated by professional societies play a vital role. They are,
1. Inspiration
2. Guidance
3. Support for responsible conduct
4. Deterring and disciplining unethical professional conduct
5. Educational and promotion of mutual understanding
6. Contributing to positive public image of profession
7. Protecting the status quo suppressing dissent within the profession and
8. Promoting business interest through restraint of trade.

Limitation of codes:
The four major limitations of codes of ethics are as follows:
1. Codes of ethics are broad guidelines, restricted to general and vague wordings/phrases. The codes cannot be applied directly to all situations. Also, it is impossible to predict all aspects of moral problems that can arise in a complex, dynamic engineering profession.

2. Engineering codes often have internal conflicts, which may result in moral dilemmas. That is, several entries in codes overlap with each other, so there are internal conflicts. But the code doesn't 't provides a method for resolving these conflicts.
3. The codes cannot serve as the final moral authority for professional conduct.
4. The proliferation of codes of ethics for different of engineering gives a feeling that ethical code is relative.

Code of Ethics for Engineers

Accreditation Board for Engineering and Technology (ABET) The Fundamental Principles
Engineers shall uphold and advance the integrity, honor, and dignity of the engineering profession by:
- *using their knowledge and skill for the enhancement of the human race;*
- *being honest and impartial and serving with fidelity the public, their employers, and clients;*
- *striving to increase the competence and prestige of the engineering profession.*
- *supporting the professional and technical societies of their discipline.*

The Fundamental Cannons

Engineers shall
- *hold paramount the safety, health, and welfare of the public in the performance of their professional duties;*
- *perform service only in areas of their competence;*
- *issue public statements only in an objective and truthful manner;*
- *actin professional matters for each employer or client as faithful agents or trustees, and shall avoid conflicts of interest;*
- *build their professional reputations on the merits of their services and shall not compete unfairly with others*
- *act in such manner as to uphold and enhance the honor, integrity and dignity of the profession;*
- *continue their professional development throughout their careers, and shall provide opportunities for the professional development of those engineers under their supervision.*

CODES OF ETHICS - *ROLES OR FUNCTIONS*

1. **Inspiration and Guidance:**
   - ❖ Codes provide positive stimulus for ethical conduct and helpful guidance by using positive language.
   - ❖ Codes should be brief to be effective and hence such codes offer only general guidance.
   - ❖ Supplementary statements or guidelines to give specific directions are added by a number of societies or professional bodies.

2. **Support:**
   - ❖ Codes give positive support to those seeking to act ethically.
   - ❖ An engineer under pressure to act unethically can use one of the publicly proclaimed codes to get support for his stand on specific moral issues.
   - ❖ Codes also serve as legal support for engineers.

3. **Deterrence and discipline:**
   - ❖ Codes can be used as a basis for conducting investigations on unethical conduct.
   - ❖ They also provide a deterrent for engineers to act immorally.
   - ❖ Engineers who are punished by professional societies for proven unethical behavior by revoking the rights to practice as engineers are also subjected to public ridicule and loss of respect from colleagues and local community.
   - ❖ This helps to produce ethical conduct even though this can be viewed as a negative way of motivation.

4. **Education and mutual understanding:**
   a. The codes can be used for discussion and reflection on moral issues and thereby improve the understanding of moral responsibilities among all engineers, clients, public and good organizations.

5. **Contributing to the profession's public image:**
   a. Codes present the engineering profession as an ethically committed society in the eyes of the public thus enhancing their image.

6. **Protecting status quo:**
   a. Codes establish ethical conventions, which can help promote an agreed upon minimum level of ethical conduct.

7. **Promoting business interests:**
   a. Codes can place unwarranted restraints of commerce on business dealings.

Relative importance of the various functions of codes of ethics

a. The perspective of engg as social experimentation clearly emphasizes the primary role 'supportive function' of the codes of ethics. This is so because, only this support enables engineers, speak out clearly and openly their views, to those affected by engg projects.
b. The, 'inspiration and guidance' and 'educative' functions are also important in promoting mutual understanding and in motivating engineers to act with higher moral standards.
c. The 'disciplinary' function in engg codes is of secondary importance. Those with unethical conduct when exposed are subject to law. Developing elaborate paralegal procedures within professional societies duplicates a function which can be done better by legal system. At best, codes should try to discipline engineers in areas which are not covered by law.
d. The worst abuse of codes has been to restrict honest moral effort in the name of 'preserving profession's public image' and 'protecting status quo'. The best way to increase trust is by encouraging and aiding engineers to speak freely and responsibly about public safety.

2.4 INDUSTRIAL STANDARDS

Industrial standards are important for any industry. Specification helps in achieving interchangeability. Standardization reduces the production costs and at the same time, the quality is achieved easily. It helps the manufacturer, customers and the public, in keeping competitiveness and ensuring quality simultaneously. Industrial standards are established by the Bureau of Indian Standards, in our country in consultation with leading industries and services. International standards have become relevant with the development of the world trade. The International Standards Organization has now detailed specifications for generic products/services with procedures that the manufacturers or service providers should follow to assure the quality of their products or service. ISO 9000-2000 series are typical examples in this direction.

Table 2.5 gives a list of some types of standards with a few examples.

Table 2.5 Industrial standards

Aspects	Purpose	Examples
1. Quality	Value appropriate to price	Surface finish of a plate, life of a motor
2. Quality of service	Assurance of product to ISO Procedures	Quality of degrees according Institutions by educational institutions
3. Safety	To safeguard against injury or damage to Property	Methods of waste disposal
4. Uniformity of physical properties and functions	Interchangeability, ease of assembly	Standard bolts and nuts, standard Time

2.5 A BALANCED OUTLOOK ON LAW

The 'balanced outlook on law' in engineering practice stresses the necessity of laws and regulations and also their limitations in directing and controlling the engineering practice. Laws are necessary because, people are not fully responsible by themselves and because of the competitive nature of the free enterprise, which does not encourage moral initiatives. Laws are needed to provide a minimum level of compliance.

The following codes are typical examples of how they were enforced in the past:

a. Code for Builders by Hammurabi

Hummurabi the king of Babylon in 1758 framed the following code for the builders: "If a builder has built a house for a man and has not made his work sound and the house which he has built has fallen down and caused the death of the householder, that builder shall be put to death. If it causes the death of the householder's son, they shall put that builder's son to death. If it causes the death of the householder's slave, he shall give slave for slave to the householder. If it destroys property, he shall replace anything it has destroyed; and because he has not made the house sound which he has built and it has fallen down, he shall rebuild the house which has fallen down from his own property. If a builder has built a house for a man and does not make his work perfect and the wall bulges, that builder shall put that wall in sound condition at his own cost" This code was expected to put in self-regulation seriously in those years.

b. Steam Boat Code in USA

Whenever there is crisis, we claim that there ought to be law to control this. Whenever there is a fire accident in a factory or fire cracker's store house or boat cap size we make this claim, and soon forget. Laws are meant to be interpreted for minimal compliance. On the other hand, laws when amended or updated continuously, would be counterproductive. Laws will always lag behind the technological development. The regulatory or inspection agencies such as Environmental authority of India can play a major role by framing rules and enforcing compliance. In the early 19th century, a law was passed in USA to provide for inspection of the safety of boilers and engines in ships. It was amended many times and now the standards formulated by the American Society of Mechanical Engineers are followed.

c. Proper Role of Laws

Good laws when enforced effectively produce benefits. They establish minimal standards of professional conduct and provide a motivation to people. Further they serve as moral support and defense for the people who are willing to act ethically.

Thus, it is concluded that:

1. The rules which govern engineering practice should be construed as of responsible experimentation rather than rules of a game. This makes the engineer responsible for the safe conduct of the experiment.
2. Precise rules and sanctions are suitable in case of ethical misconduct that involves the violation of established engineering procedures, which are aimed at the safety and the welfare of the public.
3. In situations where the experimentation is large and time consuming, the rules must not try to cover all possible outcomes, and they should not compel the engineers to follow rigid courses of action.
4. The regulation n should be broad, but make engineers accountable for their decisions, and

Through their professional societies, the engineers can facilitate framing the rules, amend wherever necessary, and enforce them, but without giving-in for conflicts of interest.

2.6 CASE STUDY: THE CHALLENGER

What happened?
The orbiter of the Challenger had three main engines fuelled by liquid hydrogen. The fuel was carried in an external fuel tank which was jettisoned when empty. During lift-off, the main engines fire for about nine minutes, although initially the thrust was provided by the two booster rockets. These booster rockets are of the solid fuel type, each burning a million-pound load of aluminum, potassium chloride, and iron oxide.

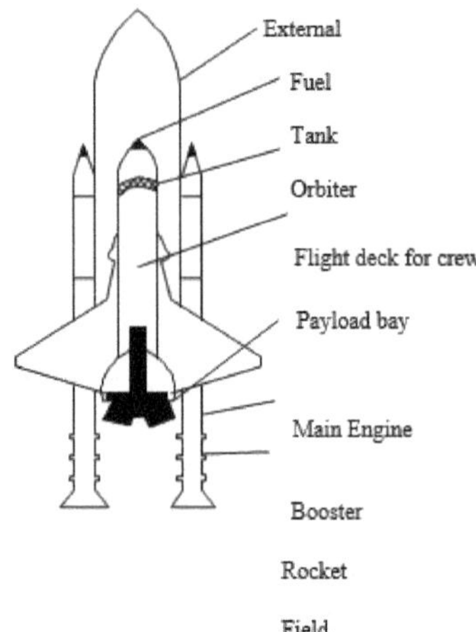

The casing of each booster rocket is about 150 feet long and 12 feet in diameter. This consists of cylindrical segments that are assembled at the launch site. There are four-field joints and they use seals consisting of pairs of O's- rings made of vulcanized rubber. The O-rings work with a putty barrier made of zinc chromate.

The engineers were employed with Rockwell International (manufacturers for the orbiter and main rocket), **Morton-Thiokol** (maker of booster rockets), and they worked for NASA. After many postponements, the launch of Challenger was set for morning of Jan 28, 1986. **Allan J. McDonald** was an engineer from Morton-Thiokol and the director of the Solid Rocket Booster Project. He was skeptic about the freezing temperature conditions forecast for that morning, which was lower than the previous launch conditions. A teleconference between NASA engineers and MT engineers was arranged by Allan.

Arnold Thompson and Roger Boisjoly, the seal experts at MT explained to the other engineers how the booster rocket walls would bulge upon launch and combustion gases can blow past the O-rings of the field joints.

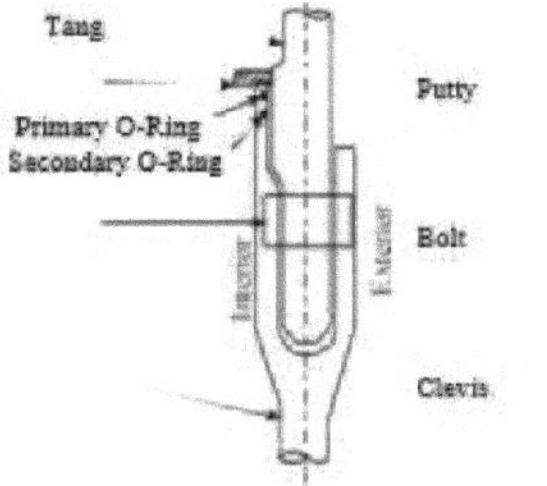

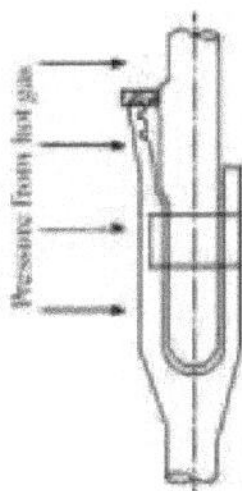

On many of the previous flights the rings have been found to have charred and eroded. In freezing temperature, the rings and the putty packing are less pliable. From the past data gathered, at temperature less than 65 $^\circ$F the O- rings failure was certain. But these data were not deliberated at that conference as the launch time was fast approaching.

The engineering managers Bob Lund and Joe Kilminster agreed that there was a safety problem. Boisjoly testified and recommended that no launch should be attempted with temperature less than 53 $^\circ$F. These managers were annoyed to postpone the launch yet again. The top management of MT was planning for the renewal of contract with NASA, for making booster rocket. The managers told Bob Lund "to take-off the engineering hat and put on your management hat". The judgment of the engineers was not given weightage. The inability of these engineers to substantiate that the launch would be unsafe was taken by NASA as an approval by Rockwell to launch.

At 11.38 a.m. the rockets along with Challenger rose up the sky. The cameras recorded smoke coming out of one of the filed joints on the right booster rocket. Soon there was a flame that hit the external fuel tank. At 76 seconds into the flight, the Challenger at a height of 10 miles was totally engulfed in a fireball. The crew cabin fell into the ocean killing all the seven aboard.

Some of the factual issues, conceptual issues and moral/normative issues in the space shuttle challenger incident, are highlighted hereunder for further study.

Moral/Normative Issues
1. The crew had no escape mechanism. Douglas, the engineer, designed an abort module to allow the separation of the orbiter, triggered by a field-joint leak. Butsucha's safe exit' was rejected as too expensive, and because of an accompanying reduction in payload.
2. The crew were not informed of the problems existing in the field joints. The principle of informed consent was not followed.
3. Engineers gave warning signals on safety. But the management group prevailed over and ignored the warning.

Conceptual Issues
1. NASA counted that the probability of failure of the craft was one in one lakh launches. But it was expected that only the 100000th launch will fail.

2. There were 700 criticality-1 items, which included the field joints. A failure in any one of them would have caused the tragedy. No back-up or stand-bye had been provided for these criticality-1 components.

Factual/Descriptive Issues
1. Field joints gave way in earlier flights. But the authorities felt the risk is not high.
2. NASA has disregarded warnings about the bad weather, at the time of launch, because they wanted to complete the project, prove their supremacy, get the funding from Government continued and get an applaud from the President of USA.

The inability of the Rockwell Engineers (manufacturer) to prove that the lift-off was unsafe. This was interpreted by the NASA, as an approval by Rockwell to launch

2.7 ENGINEERING EXPERIMENTS WITH STANDARD EXPERIMENTS

There are many similarities and differences between engineering experiments and other standard experiments.

Similarity to Standard Experiments:
1. There are many aspects of engineering that make it appropriate to view engineering projects as experiments. The three important aspects are as follows:
2. Engineering projects, like the standard experiments, are carried out in partial uncertainties. The uncertainties may include in the,
   - ✓ Design calculation
   - ✓ Exact properties of raw materials used
   - ✓ Constancies of material processing and fabrication
   - ✓ Nature of working of final products
3. The final outcomes of engineering projects are also generally uncertain like those of other experiments. For, example, a nuclear reactor may reveal unexpected problems that endangered the surrounding people.
4. Similar to standard experiments, engineering experiments also requires thorough knowledge about the products at the pre-production and post-production stages. Thus engineering, like any other experimentation, requires constant monitoring, alertness, and vigil on the part of the engineers at every stage of the project.

Contrast with standard experiments:
The study of knowing differences between engineering and other standard experiments is helpful to the engineers to realize their special and moral responsibility. Some aspects of these differences are given bellow:

1. **Experimental control:**
   - ✓ Experimental control is the most important difference between engineering and other standard experiments.
   - ✓ In standard experiments, experimental control involves selecting members for two different groups randomly. The first group members are given the special,

experimental treatment, whereas the members of other group are not given that special treatment control, as they own the authority of that project. So here the experimental subjects say clients or end-users are out of experimenter 's control. In this type, it is not possible to select the member from various group randomly. Instead the engineers should work with the available historical and fair data about various groups randomly. Instead, the engineering should work the available historical and fair data about various groups that uses the end product.

The above discussion also justifies the view of engineering as a social experimentation.

2. Informed consent:
    ✓ It is known that there is always a strong human interface in the use of the engineering experiments 'result; and also the beneficiaries are invariably humans. Therefore, engineering experiments are also viewed at par the medical experiments.
    ✓ When a medicine or an engineering product is to be tested on a person, then the moral and legal rights is to get _informed consent 'for him. Informed consent consists of two main elements:
        1. Knowledge: The human subjects should be given all the information to make a reasonable decision.
        2. Voluntariness: The human subjects should show their willingness to be a human model voluntarily. The person should not be forced, deceived, fraud, etc.
    ✓ The manufacturer of the should give all the information about the potential risks and benefits of their products to their customers and users.
    ✓ The characteristics of a valid consent '

The informed consent is called as _valid consent 'when the following three conditions are met:
        1. The consent should be given voluntarily and not by force.
        2. The consent should be based on all information needed for the rational person to make reasonable decision.
        3. The consentient should be physically and mentally fit; then he should be major i.e., above 18years.

UNIT- 3
ENGINEERS RESPONSIBILITY FOR SAFETY

3.1 SAFETY AND RISK

Imagine you are a fresh graduate.
- You get a job as an engineer in a large atomic power plant.

43

- Would you take it or not?
- Under what conditions would you take it?
- Under what conditions would you not?
- Why?

People as Consumers:
- Active Consumers: directly involve themselves e.g., mowing the lawn, washing clothes or toasting bread.
- Passive Consumers: have less choice and less control e.g., Water, Electricity, Petrol,
- Bystanders: e.g., exposed to Pollution from unknown sources

What is safe to Entrepreneurs, may not be so to Engineers. e.g., Pilots: "Indian Airports are not safe; Low Vision in Fog—. What is safe to Engineers, may not be so to Public. e.g., Top loading WashingMachineTypicallyseveralgroupsofpeopleareinvolvedinsafetymattersbuthavetheir own interests at stake. Each group may differ in what is safe and what is not.

Concept of Safety

A ship in harbor is safe, but that is not what ships are built for‖– John A. Shed 2. A thing is safe if its risks are judged to be acceptable"-William W. Lawrence
- We buy an ill-designed Iron box in a sale-> Underestimating risk
- We judge fluoride in water can kill lots of people -> Overestimating risk
- We hire a taxi, without thinking about its safety -> Not estimating risk
- How does a judge pass a judgement on safety in these 3cases?

So, this definition won't do in real life. Then, what is acceptable also depends upon the individual or group's value judgment. Hence a better, working definition of concept of safety could be,—A thing is safe (to a certain degree)with respect to a given person or group at a given time if, were they fully aware of its risks and expressing their most settled values, they would judge those risks to be acceptable (to that certain degree).‖-

Mike Martin and Roland Schinzinger

A thing is NOTSAFE if it exposes us to unacceptable danger or hazard. RISK is the potential that something unwanted and harmful may occur. We take a risk when we under take something or use a product that is not safe. Risk in technology could include dangers of bodily harm, economic loss, or environmental degradation. Some may assume that —safety is a concrete concept, while —risk‖ is a vague, hypothetical concept
- In fact, it's the other way around
- Risks always exist. But true safety never exists, except in hypothetical situations
- So, risk is reality, safety is fantasy.

What degree of risk is acceptable?

Safety is a matter of how people would find risks acceptable or unacceptable, if they knew the risks, and are basing their judgments on their most settled value perspective.

So, to this extent, it is objective. Perspectives differ. To this extent, it is subjective. So, Safety is 'acceptable risk'.

Acceptable Risk

A risk is acceptable when those affected are generally no longer (or not) apprehensive about it. Apprehension (i.e. anxiety) depends largely on factors such as

- whether the risk is assumed voluntarily.
- how the probabilities of harm (or benefit) are perceived.
- job-related or other pressures that causes people to be aware of or to overlook risks.
- whether the defects of a risky activity or situation are immediately noticeable or close at hand.
- whether the potential victims are identifiable beforehand.

<u>3.2</u> ASSESMENT OF SAFETY AND RISK

The manner in which information necessary for decision making is presented can greatly influence how risks are perceived. Consider this example: In a particular case of disaster management, the only options available are provided in 2 different ways to the public for one to be chosen (where lives of 600 people are at stake).

Alternate 1

If program A is followed, 200 people will be saved. If Program B is followed, 1/3 probability is 600 people will be saved and 2/3 probability that nobody will be saved.

Response

72% of the target group chose option A and 28% option B

Alternate 2

If program A is followed, 400 people will die. If Program B is followed, 1/3 probability is that nobody will die and 2/3 probability that 600 people will die.

Response

This time only 22% of the target group chose option A and 78% option B

Conclusion:

1. The option perceived as yielding firm gain will tend to be preferred over those from which gains are perceived as risky or only probable.
2. Option emphasizing firm losses will tend to be avoided in favor of those whose chances of success are perceived as probable.

Secondary Costs of Products

- Cost of products is High, if designed unsafely
- Returns and Warranty Expenses
- Loss of Customer Goodwill

- Cost of litigation
- Loss of Customers due to injuries in using it
- Cost of rework, lost time in attending to design problems Manufacturer's understanding of the risk in a product is necessary
- To help reduce secondary costs
- To know the possible risk for purposes of pricing, disclaimers, legal terms and conditions, etc.
- To know the cost of reducing the risks
- To take a decision before finalizing the design.

Buyer's understanding of the risk in a product is necessary:
- To judge whether he/she wants to take the risks
- To judge whether the „risk vs. costs" justifies taking the risk

3.3.RISK BENEFIT ANALYSIS

Ethical Implications
- When is someone entitled to impose a risk on another in view of a supposed benefit to others?
- Consider the worst-case scenarios of persons exposed to maximum risks while they are reaping only minimum benefits. Are their rights violated? Are they provided safer alternatives?
- Engineers should keep in mind that risks to known persons are perceived differently from statistical risks
- Engineers may have no control over grievance redressal.

Conceptual difficulties in Risk-Benefit Analysis.
Both risks and benefits lie in future
- Heavy discounting of future because the very low present values of cost/benefits do not give a true picture of future sufferings.
- Both have related uncertainties but difficult to arrive at expected values
- What if benefits accrue to one party and risks to another?
- Can we express risks & benefits in a common set of units?
- Risks can be expressed in one set of units (deaths on the highway) and benefits in another (speed of travel)?

Many projects, which are highly beneficial to the public, have to be safe also. Hence these projects can be justified using RISK-BENEFIT analysis. In these studies, one should find out.
    a. What are the risks involved?
    b. What are the benefits that would accrue?
    c. When would benefits be derived and when risks have to be faced?
    d. Who are the ones to be benefited and who are the ones subjected to risk-are they the same set of people or different? The issue here is not, say, cost-effective design but it is

only cost of risk-taking Vs benefit analysis. Engineers should first recommend the project feasibility based on risk- benefit analysis and once it is justified, then they may get into cost-effectiveness without increasing the risk visualized. In all this, engineers should ask themselves this ethical question: Under what conditions, is someone in society entitled to impose a risk on someone else on behalf of a supposed benefit to others.

3.4 REDUCING RISK

1. Application of inherent safety concept in design eg, LPG cylinder is provided with frame to protect the valve while handling and facilitates cryogenic storage. A magnetic door catch provides an easy escape for children caught inside the fridge accidently.
2. Case of redundancy principle in the instrument protection/ design. For example, use of use of standby device and back up for computer storage.
3. Periodical monitoring (inspection) and testing of safety system to ensure reliability, eg, fire extinguishers, 'earth' system in electric circuits are checked periodically.
4. Issue of operation manuals, training of the operating personnel and regular audits are adopted to ensure that the procedures are understood, followed and the systems are kept in working condition.
5. Development of well-designed emergency evacuation plan and regular rehearsal/drills to ensure preparedness, in case of emergency.

3.5 CHERNOBYL CASE STUDIES AND BHOPAL

3.5.1   CHERNOBYL CASESTUDY

What Happened?

At 1:24 AM on April 26, 1986, there was an explosion at the Soviet nuclear power plant at Chernobyl. One of their actors overheated, igniting a pocket of hydrogen gas. The explosion blew the top off the containment building, and exposed the molten reactor to the air. Thirty-one power plant workers were killed in the initial explosion, and radioactive dust and debris spewed into the air.

It took several days to put out the fire. Helicopters dropped sand and chemicals on the reactor rubble, finally extinguishing the blaze. Then the Soviets hastily buried their actor in a sarcophagus of concrete. Estimates of deaths among the clean-up workers vary widely. Four thousand clean-up workers may have died in the following weeks from the radiation.

The countries now known as Belarus and Ukraine were hit the hardest by the radioactive fallout. Winds quickly blew the toxic cloud from Eastern Europe into Sweden and Norway. Within a week, radioactive levels had jumped over all of Europe, Asia, and Canada. It is estimated that seventy-thousand Ukrainians have been disabled, and five million people were exposed to radiation. Estimates of total deaths due to radioactive contamination range from 15,000 to 45,000 or more.

To give you an idea of the amount of radioactive material that escaped, the atomic bomb dropped on Hiroshima had a radioactive mass of four and a half tons. The exposed radioactive mass at Chernobyl was fifty tons.

In the months and years following, birth defects were common for animals and humans. Even the leaves on the trees became deformed.

Today, in Belarus and Ukraine, thyroid cancer and leukemia are still higher than normal. The towns of Pripyat and Chernobyl in the Ukraine are ghost towns. They will be uninhabitable due to radioactive contamination for several hundred years. The worst of the contaminated area is called "The Zone," and it is fenced off. Plants, meat, milk, and water in the area are still unsafe. Despite the contamination, millions of people live in and near The Zone, too poor to move to safer surroundings.

Further, human genetic mutations created by the radiation exposure have been found in children who have only recently been born. This suggests that there may be another whole generation of Chernobyl victim. Recent reports say that there are some indications that the concrete sarcophagus at Chernobyl is breaking down.

How a Nuclear Power Plant Works

The countries now known as Belarus and Ukraine were hit the hardest by the radioactive fallout. Winds quickly blew the toxic cloud from Eastern Europe into Sweden and Norway. Within a week, radioactive levels had jumped over all of Europe, Asia, and Canada. It is estimated that seventy-thousand Ukrainians have been disabled, and five million people were exposed to radiation. Estimates of total deaths due to radioactive contamination range from 15,000 to 45,000 or more.

To give you an idea of the amount of radioactive material that escaped, the atomic bomb dropped on Hiroshima had a radioactive mass of four and a half tons. The exposed radioactive mass at Chernobyl was fifty tons.

The reactor at Chernobyl was composed of almost 200 tons of uranium. This giant block of uranium generated heat and radiation. Water ran through the hot reactor, turning to steam. The steam ran the turbines, thereby generating electricity. The hotter the reactor, the more electricity would be generated.

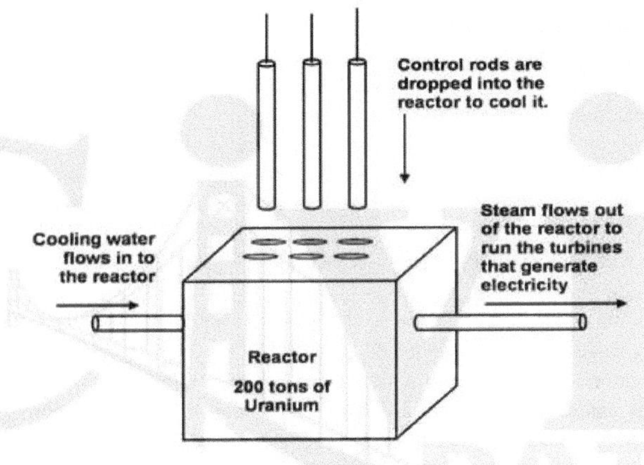

Left to itself, the reactor would become too reactive—it would become hotter and hotter and more and more radioactive. If there actor had nothing to cool it down, it would quickly meltdown—a process where the

reactor gets so hot that it melts— melting through the floor. So, engineers needed a way to control the temperature of the reactor, to keep it from the catastrophic meltdown. Further, the engineers needed to be able to regulate the temperature of the reactor—so that it ran hotter when more electricity was needed, and could run colder when less electricity was desired.

The method they used to regulate the temperature of the reactor was to insert heat- absorbing rods, called control rods. These control rods absorb heat and radiation. The rods hang above the reactor, and can be lowered into the reactor, which will cool the reactor. When more electricity is needed, the rods can be re moved from the reactor, which will allow the reactor to heat up. The reactor has hollow tubes, and the control rods are lowered into these reactor tubes, or raised up out of the reactor tubes. At the Chernobyl-type reactors, there are 211 control rods. The more control rods that are inserted, the colder the reactor runs. The more control rods that are removed, the hotter the reactor becomes.

Soviet safety procedures demanded that at least 28 rods were inserted into the Chernobyl reactor at all times. This was a way to make sure that the reactor wouldn't overheat.

Water was another method to moderate the temperature of the reactor. When more water ran through the reactor, the reactor cooled faster. When less water ran through the reactor, the reactor stayed hot.

CHERNOBYL NEAR KIEY. RUSSIA (APRIL 1986)

The RBMK (Acronym for water cooled and graphite moderated) reactors were graphite moderated and they use water tubes. A test on the turbine generator was planned to be conducted during a scheduled plant shut-down maintenance.

To conduct the test, the power plant output was reduced to 700 MW. But due to a sudden and unexpected demand, the power output has to be raised.

1. To go ahead with the test, the reactor operators had already disconnected the emergency core-cooling system, ignoring the raise in demand situation.
2. Further, a control device was not properly reprogrammed to maintain power at 700-100 MW level
3. The test was conducted at 200 MW power out-put which is very low for the test. They should have shut down the reactor.
4. The operators blocked all emergency signals and automatic shut-down controls, thus all safety systems were disconnected.
5. The operators raised control rods to increase power output and tried to continue the test. This made the reactor unsafe. The temperature of RBMK reactor increased and the fission rate increased.
6. The test should have been postponed but continued. The reactor core melted and due to the Hydrogen accumulation, the reactor caught fire and the radioactive waste began to spread out in USSR and also Europe.

The people living around were informed after a few hours and were evacuated 12 hours after the explosion. More than 30 workers in the complex lost their lives, while 200 workers sustained burns. About 8000 people lost their lives. The agricultural products were affected due to contaminated radioactive water, for several years.

SAFETY LESSONS FROM TMI AND CHERNOBYL

1. The thickness of the containment should be more, to withstand the possible explosion and further damage due to radiation and leakage over the surroundings (Chernobyl).
2. When the test began at low loads, the demand for increased outpower should have been declined.
3. Or the tests should have been abandoned and all control switched on. Then the output should have been increased (Chernobyl)
4. The decision making on the test and increase the load should have been with one person or the decision makers should have coordinated with each other. (Chernobyl 1)
5. Values are the least-reliable components in the hydraulic system. Such a malfunction of the pressure relief valve and lack of information about its opening (or closing) were reported else wherein the past. But there was no 'learning from the past (TMI)
6. Continuous monitoring of the components such as demineralizer and pressure operated relief valve must have been made (TMI).
7. A comprehensive precursor program (emergency procedure) should have been implemented to record a few incidents sequence and map these events to risk models.

The mapping based on technical and human factors give us accounts, how people react and interact under conditions of stress (TMI).

8. Periodical mock drills of emergency for the operators (Safe exit) should have been arranged (TMI and Chernobyl 1)
9. In-stack radioactivity monitoring instrument indicated a rise earlier. The operators at TMI 2 should have been informed the superior at once. People residing in the neighborhood ought to have been informed and steps initiated to evacuated the public immediately (TMI especially and also Chernobyl)

3.5.2 BHOPAL GAS TRAGEDY

On December 3, 1984, Union Carbide's pesticide-manufacturing plant in Bhopal, India leaked 40 tons of the deadly gas, methyl is ocyanate into a sleeping, impoverished community -killing2,500 within a few days, 10000 permanently disabled and injuring 100,000 people. Ten years later, it increased to 4000 to 7000 deaths and injuries to600,000.

Risks taken:

- Storage tank of Methyl Isocyanate gas was filled to more than 75% capacity as against Union Carbide's spec. that it should never be more than 60%full.
- The company's West Virginia plant was controlling the safety systems and detected leakagesthro"computersbuttheBhopalplantonlyusedmanuallabourforcontrolandleak detection.
- The Methyl Isocyanate gas, being highly concentrated, burns parts of body with which it comes into contact, even blinding eyes and destroying lungs.

Causal Factors:
- Three protective systems out of service
- Plant was understaffed due to costs.
- Very high inventory of MIC, an extremely toxic material.
- The accident occurred in the early morning.
- Most of the people killed lived in a shanty (poorly built) town located very close to the plant fence.

Workers made the following attempts to save the plant:
- They tried to turn on the plant refrigeration system to cool down the environment and slow the reaction. (The refrigeration system had been drained of coolant weeks before and never refilled- it cost too much.)
- They tried to route expanding gases to a neighboring tank. (The tank's pressure gauge was broken and indicated the tank was full when it was really empty.)
- They tried to purge the gases through a scrubber. (The scrubber was designed for flow rates, temperatures and pressures that were a fraction of what was by this time escaping from the tank.

The scrubber was as a result ineffective.
- They tried to route the gases through a flare tower -- to burn them away. (The supply line to the flare tower was broken and hadn't been replaced.)

• They tried to spray water on the gases and have them settle to the ground, by this time the chemical reaction was nearly completed. (The gases were escaping at a point 120 feet above ground; the hoses were designed to shoot water up to 100 feet into the air.) In just 2 hours the chemicals escaped to form a deadly cloud over hundreds of thousands of people incl. poor migrant laborer's who stayed close to the plant.

3.6 DIFFICULTIES IN ESTABLISHING SAFE GUARDS

Difficulties in establishing Safeguards:
- Incomplete knowledge of the engineering subject
- Refusal to face hard questions caused by lack of knowledge
- False sense of security
- e.g. Nuclear waste disposal problem
- Caution in stating probabilities of rare events
- Varying understanding of risk based on presentation of facts
- Risk assessments based on incorrect/unacceptable assumptions/data
- Only a few persons/groups participate in the exercise
- Some of the ways by which engineers may try to reduce risks.
- In all the areas of works, engineers should give top priority for product safety.
- They should believe that accidents are caused by dangerous conditions that can be corrected. Negligence and operator errors are not the principal causes of accidents.
- If a product is made safe, the initial costs need not be high if safety is built into a product from the beginning. It is the design changes done at a later date that are costly. Even then life cycle costs can be made lower for the redesigned or retrofitted product (for safety).
- If safety is not built into the original design, people can be hurt during testing stage itself.
- They should get out of the thinking that warnings about hazards are adequate and that insurance coverage is cheaper than planning for safety.
- All it takes to make a product safe is to have different perspective on the design problem with emphasis on safety.
- Examples of Improved Safety
- Magnetic door catch introduced on refrigerators
- Prevent death by asphyxiation of children accidentally trapped inside
- The catch now permits the door to opened from inside easily
- Cheaper than older types of latches
- Dead-man Handle for Drivers in trains
- Semaphore signaling
- Volkswagen's car safety belt
- Attachment on the door so that belt automatically goes in place on Entry

UNIT-4
RESPONSIBILITIES AND RIGHTS

4.1 COLLEGIALITY AND LOYALTY

Collegiality is a kind of connectedness grounded in respect for professional expertise and in a commitment to the goals and values of the profession and as such, collegiality includes a disposition to support and co-operate with one's colleagues".- Craig Ihara. The central elements of collegiality are respect, commitment, connectedness and cooperation.
Respect: Acknowledge the worth of other engineers engaged in producing socially useful and safe products.
Commitment: Share a devotion to the moral ideals inherent in the practice of engineering.
Connectedness: Aware of being part of a co-operative undertaking created by shared commitments and expertise. Collegiality, like most virtues, can be misused and distorted. It should not be reduced to,, group interest "but should be a shared devotion for public good. It is not defaming colleagues, but it does not close the eyes to unethical practices of the co-professionals, either.

Classifications of Loyalty
- Agency-Loyalty
- Fulfill one's contractual duties to an employer.
- Duties are particular tasks for which one is paid
- Co-operating with colleagues
- Following legitimate authority within the organization.
- Identification-Loyalty:
- It has to do with attitudes, emotions and a sense of personal identity.
- Seeks to meet one's moral duties with personal attachment and affirmation.
- It is against detesting their employers and companies, and do work reluctantly and horribly (this is construed as disloyalty)

This means
- Avoid conflicts of interest,
- Inform employers of any possible conflicts of interest,
- Protect confidential information,
- Be honest in making estimates,
- Admit one's errors, etc.

Loyalty - Obligation of Engineers
- Agency-Loyalty
- Engineers are hired to do their duties.
- Hence obligated to employers within proper limits
- Identification-Loyalty
- Obligatory on two conditions;
1. When some important goals are met by and through a group in which the engineers participate

53

2. When employees are treated fairly, receiving the share of benefits and burdens.
3. But clearly, identification-loyalty is a virtue and not strictly an obligation.

4.2 RESPECT FOR AUTHORITY

    a. Allowing everyone to exercise *uncontrolled individual discretion creates chaos (confusion)*

    b. Clear lines of authority identify areas of personal responsibility and accountability.

Need for Authority
Authority is needed since

    a) Allowing everyone to exercise *uncontrolled individual discretion creates chaos* (confusion).

    b) Clear lines of authority *identify areas of* personal responsibility and *accountability.*

Institutional Authority and Expert Authority
Institutional authority
'The institutional right given to a person to exercise power based on the resources of the institution'.

    o It is acquired, exercised and defined within in situations.

    o It is given to individuals to perform their institutional duties assigned within the organization. There is not always a perfect match between the authority granted and the qualifications needed to exercise it.

Expert authority
'The possession of special knowledge, skill or competence to perform some task or to give sound advice'.

Engineers may have expert authority but their institutional authority, *may only be,* to *provide management* with analysis of possible ways to perform a technical task, after which they are *restricted to following management's directive* about which option to pursue. In large companies, *engineers, advisors and consultants* in staff function carry *expert authority,* while *institutional authority* is vested only with *line managers.*

Authority Vs Power

Ineffective persons, even if vested with authority by their institution, *may not be able to summon* the power their position allows them to exercise. On the other hand, people who are *effective* may be *able to wield greater power* that goes beyond the authority attached to the positions they hold. Highly respected engineers of proven integrity belong to this class.

Authority - Morally justified
Observations on authority.

o   An *employer* who has institutional authority may *direct engineers* to do something that is *not morally justified.*
o   Engineers may feel that they have an institutional *duty too bey* directive that is *morally unjustified, but* their moral *duty*, all things considered, *is not too bey.*

o   To decide whether a specific act of *exercising institutional authority is morally justified*, we need to know whether the institutional *goals are* themselves *morally permissible* or desirable and whether that *act violates* basic moral duties.

'Zone Of Acceptance' of Authority

'A subordinate is said to accept authority whenever he permits his behavior to be guided by the decision of a superior, without independently examining the merits of that decision'-Herbert Simon
o   Simon notes that all employees tend to have a *'zone of acceptance'* in which they are willing to accept their employer's authority.
o   *Within that zone*, an individual, relaxing his own critical faculties, *permits* the decision of the *employer to guide* him.
o   Employees generally *do not make an issue* of questionable incidents on morality, *out of a sense of responsibility* to give their employer leeway within which to operate and often *not to risk their jobs*.
o   The *problem increases* when employees slowly *expand* the boundaries of *tolerance and rationalize* it.

This only shows that engineers should *never stop* critically *reviewing* the employer's *directives* especially *on moral issues*.

<u>4.3</u> COLLECTIVE BARGAINING AND OCCUPATIONAL

Collective bargaining is inconsistent with loyalty to employers because it
- is against the desires of the employer
- uses force or coercion against the employer and
- involves collective and organized opposition.

But every instance of such conduct need not be unethical. An example: Three engineers sincerely feel that they are underpaid. After their representations to their bosses are in vain, they threaten their employer, politely, that they would seek employment elsewhere. Here, even though, they act against the desires of their employer and have acted collectively, they have not acted unethically or violated their duty.

- Public Service Argument"- Collective bargaining.
- Public Service Argument" is an argument against collective bargaining.
- The paramount duty of engineers is to serve the public.

- Unions, by definition, promote the interests of their members and whenever there is a clash of interests, the interest of the general public is ignored by them. Though the argument is a valid one, It looks at the worst possible scenarios with unions and decides that engineering unions act only irresponsibly.
- A body of engineers can promote engineers" interest within limits set by professional concern for the public good.

Benefits of Collective Bargaining.

a) Unions have created healthy salaries and high standard of living of employees.
b) They give a sense of participation in company decision making.
c) They are a good balance to the power of employers to fire employees at will.
d) They provide an effective grievance redressal procedure for employee complaints.

Harms Caused by Collective Bargaining.

a) Unions are devastating the economy of a country, being a main source of inflation
b) With unions, there is no congenial (friendly), cooperative decision making.
c) Unions do not promote quality performance by making job promotion and retention based on seniority.
d) They encourage unrest and strained relations between employees and employers.

4.4 CONFIDENTIALITY

Confidentiality is an ethical principle associated with several professions (e.g., medicine, law, religion, professional psychology, and journalism). In ethics, and (in some places) in law and alternative forms of legal dispute resolution such as mediation, some types of communication between a person and one of these professionals are "privileged" and may not be discussed or divulged to third parties. In those jurisdictions in which the law makes provision for such confidentiality, there are usually penalties for its violation

Confidentiality or confidential information:
- Information considered desirable to be kept secret.
- Any information that the employer or client would like to have kept secret in order to compete effectively against business rivals.
- This information includes how business is run, its products, and suppliers, which directly affects the ability of the company to compete in the marketplace
- Helps the competitor to gain advantage or catchup Privileged information, Proprietary information and Patents:

Privileged information:
- Informationavailableonlyonthebasisofspecialprivilege"suchasgrantedtoanemployee working on a special assignment.

Proprietary information:

- Information that a company owns or is the proprietor of.
- This is primarily used in legal sense.
- Also called Trade Secret. A trade secret can be virtually any type of information that has not become public and which an employer has taken steps to keep secret.

Patents:.
- Legally protect specific products from being manufactured and sold by competitors without the express permission of the patentholder.
- Theyhavethedrawbackofbeingpublicandcompetitorsmayeasilyworkaroundthemby creating alternate designs.
- Differ from trade secrets

Obligation of Confidentiality:
1. Based on ordinary moral considerations:
a. Respect for autonomy:
- Recognizing the legitimate control over private information (individuals or corporations).
- This control is required to maintain their privacy and protect their self-interest.

b. Respect for Promise:
- Respecting promises in terms of employment contracts not to divulge certain information considered sensitive by the employer

c. Regard for public wellbeing:
- Only when there is a confidence that the physician will not reveal information, the patient will have the trust to confide in him.
- Similarly, only when companies maintain some degree of confidentiality concerning their products, the benefits of competitiveness within a free market are promoted.

2. Based on Major Ethical Theories:
- All theories profess that employers have moral and institutional rights to decide what information about their organization should be released publicly.
- They acquire these rights as part of their responsibility to protect the interest of the organization.
- All the theories, rights ethics, duty ethics and utilitarianism justify this confidentiality but in different ways.

3. Effect of Change of Job on Confidentiality:
- Employees are obliged to protect confidential information regarding former employment, after a change of job.
- The confidentiality trust between employer and employee continues beyond the period of employment.
- But the employee cannot be forced not to seek a change of job.
- The employer 's right to keep the trade secrets confidential by a former employee should be accepted at the same time, the employee's right to seek career advancement cannot also be denied.

<u>**4.5**</u> **CONFLICTS OF INTEREST**

Conflict of Interest **arises when two conditions are met:**

1. The professional is in a relationship or a role that requires exercising good judgment on behalf of the interests of an employer or client and
2. The professional has some additional or side interest that could threaten good judgment in serving the interests of the employee or client. E.g., *When an engineer is paid based on a percentage of the cost of the design and there is no incentive for him to cut costs-* The distrust caused by this situation compromises the engineers' ability to cut costs and calls into question his judgement

'An act of gift' and 'An act of bribe'

'A *gift* is a *bribe* if you can't *eat, drink or smoke it in a day*'.

'If you think that your offer of acceptance of a particular gift would have *grave* or merely *embarrassing consequences for your company if made public*, then the gift should be considered a bribe'.

'*Bribe* can be said to be a *substantial* amount of money or goods offered beyond a stated business contract with the *aim of winning an advantage* in gaining or keeping the contract'.

Here '*substantial*' means that which is *sufficient to distort the judgment* of a typical person.

CONFLICT OF INTEREST CREATED BY INTEREST IN OTHER COMPANIES

- When one *works actually for the competitor* or subcontractor as an employee or consultant
- *Having partial ownership or substantial stock holdings in the competitor's business.*
- *It may not arise by merely having a spouse working for sub-contractor to one's company, but it will arise if one's job also includes granting contracts to that subcontractor*
- *Tempting customers away from their current employer, while still working for them to form their own competing business*
- *Moonlighting usually creates conflicts when working for competitors, suppliers or customers but does not conflict when working for others without affecting the present employer's business*
- *'Moonlighting' means working in one's spare time for another employer*

CONFLICTS OF INTEREST CREATED BY INSIDER INFORMATION

o *Using inside information* to *set-up a business* opportunity for *oneself or family or friends.*

o *Buying stock* in the company for which one works is *not objectionable* but it should be based on the *same information* available to the public.

o The *use* of any company *secrets* by employee to *secure a personal gain* threatens the interest of the company.

AVOIDING CONFLICTS OF INTERESTS

o Taking guidance from *Company Policy*

o In the absence of such a policy taking a *second opinion from a coworker or manager.* This gives an impression that there no intension on the part of the engineer to hide anything.

o In the absence of either of these options, to *examine ones own motives* and *use the ethical* problem solving *techniques.*

o One can look carefully into the professional codes of ethics *which uniformly forbid conflicts of interest.* Some of these codes have very explicit statements that can help determine whether or not the situation constitutes conflict of interest.

<u>4.6</u> OCCUPATIONAL CRIME

TYPE OF CRIME

➢ *Domestic crime:* Non-accidental crime committed *by members* of the family

➢ *Professional Crime:* When crime is *pursued as a profession* or day to day occupation

➢ *Blue collar crime (or) Street crime:* Crime *against person, property* (theft, assault on a person, rape)

➢ *Victimless crime:* Person *who commits* the crime *is the victim* of the crime. E.g. Drug addiction

➢ *Hate crime:* Crime done on the banner of *religion, community, linguistics*

OCCUPATIONAL CRIME

a. **Occupational crimes are *illegal acts* made possible through one's *lawful employment.***

b. **It is the *secretive violation of laws* regulating work activities.**

c. **When committed by office workers or professionals, occupational crime is called *'white collar crime'.***

People Committing Occupational Crimes

➢ Usually have *high standard of education*

- ➢ From a *non-criminal family background*
- ➢ Middle class male around *27 years of age* (70% of the time) with *no previous history*
- ➢ *No involvement in drug or alcohol abuse*
- ➢ *Those who had troublesome life experience in the childhood (Blum)*
- ➢ *People without firm principles (Spencer)*
- ➢ *Firms with declining profitability (Coleman,1994)*
- ➢ *Firms in highly regulated areas and volatilemarket pharmaceutical, petroleum industry (Albanese,1995)*

PRICE FIXING

An act was passed, which forbade (prevented) companies from jointly setting prices in ways that restrain free competition and trade. Unfortunately, many senior people, well respected and positioned were of the opinion that 'price fixing' was good for their organizations and the public.

Employees Endangering Lives of Employees

Employers indulge in exposing their employees to safety hazards. They escape criminal action against them, by paying nominal compensations even if their crimes are proved in court. And even this happens only when the victim sues company for damages under civil law.

OCCUPATIONAL CRIME:

- *Occupational crimes are illegal acts made possible through one"s lawful employment.*
- *It is the secretive violation of laws regulating work activities.*
- *When committed by office workers or professionals, occupational crime is called „white collar crime".*
- *People Committing Occupational Crimes*
- *Usually have high standard of education*
- *From a non-criminal family background*
- *Middle class male around 27 years of age (70% of the time) with no previous*
- *History*
- *No involvement in drug or alcohol abuse*
- *Those who had troublesome life experience in the childhood (Blum)*
- *People without firm principles (Spencer)*
- *Firms with declining profitability (Coleman,1994)*
- *Firms in highly regulated areas and volatile market-pharmaceutical, petroleum industry. (Albanese, 1995)*

<u>4.7</u> PROFESSIONAL RIGHTS

Professional Rights & Ethical Theories

Professional rights:
- The right to form and *express one's professional judgment freely*
- The right to *refuse* to carry out *illegal and unethical activity*
- The right to *talk publicly* about one's work *within bounds* set by confidentiality obligation
- The right to *engage* in the activities of *professional societies*
- The right to *protect* the clients and the public *from the dangers* that might arise from one's work
- The right to professional *recognition* of one's services.

Right of Professional Conscience

- There is one *basic* and generic professional right of engineers, the *moral right to exercise responsible professional judgment* in pursuing professional responsibilities.
- Pursuing these responsibilities involves *exercising* both *technical judgment*
  - and *reasoned moral convictions*.
- This basic right can be referred to as *the right of professional conscience*.

Right of Conscientious Refusal

The right of Conscientious refusal is the right to *refuse to engage in unethical behavior* and to refuse to do so *solely because one views it as unethical*

Two situations to be considered.

1. Where there is widely shared agreement in profession as to whether an act is unethical
Here, professionals have a moral right to refuse to participate in such activities.

2. Where there is room for disagreement among reasonable people over whether an act is unethical.

Here, it is possible that there could be *different ethical view points* from the professional and the employer. In such cases the engineers can have a *limited right* to *turn down* assignments that violates their personal conscience *only in matters of great importance* such as threats to human life. This right also depends on the *ability* of the employer *to reassign* the engineer to alternate projects *without serious economic hardships* to the organization. The *right of professional conscience does not extend to the right to be paid for not working.*

Right to Recognition

Right to Recognition involves two parts.

The right to *reasonable remuneration* gives the moral right for fighting against corporations making good profits while engineers are being paid poorly. Also is the case where patents are not being rewarded properly by the corporations benefiting from such patents. The other *right to recognition* is non-monetary part of recognition to the work of engineers. But *what is reasonable remuneration or reasonable recognition* is a difficult question and should be resolved by discussions between employees and employers only.

1. ***Rights Ethics:***
    o The most basic human right, which needs no justification, as per A.I. Meldon, is to pursue one's legitimate (those that do not violate others' rights) interests.
    o The right to pursue legitimate interests gives a person right to pursue professional moral obligations.
    o This may be viewed as a human right of conscience directly derived from the basic human right
2. ***Duty Ethics:***
    o I have a right to something only because others have duties or obligations to allow me (and not interfere) to do so.
    o If we derive the meaning of 'others' as employers, then the basic professional right is justified by reference to others' duties to support or not interfere with the work-related exercise of conscience by professionals.
3. ***Utilitarianism:***
    o Public good can be served by allowing professionals to meet their obligations to the public.
    o These obligations arise due to the professional's role in promoting public good.
    o The basic goal of producing the most good for the greatest number of people is enough to justify the right of professional conscience.

Engineers' Moral Rights

Engineers' moral rights fall into categories of *human, employee, contractual and professional rights.*

WHISTLE-BLOWING AND ITS FEATURES

Whistle blowing is an *act of conveying information* about a *significant moral problem* by a *present or former employee, outside approved channels* (or against strong pressure) to someone, in a position to take action on the problem.

The features of *Whistle blowing* are:

- Act of Disclosure: *Intentionally conveying information outside approved organizational channels when the person is under pressure not to do so from higher- ups.*
- Topic: *The information is believed to concern a significant moral problem for the organization.*
- Agent: *The person disclosing the information is an employee or former employee.*
- Recipient: *The information is conveyed to a person or organization who can act onit.*

TYPES OF WHISTLE BLOWING

External Whistle blowing: The act of passing on information outside the organization. *Internal Whistle blowing:* The act of passing on information to someone within the organization but outside the approved channels.
Either type is likely to be considered as disloyalty, but the second one is often seen as less serious than the latter. From corporations' point of view both are serious because it leads to distrust, disharmony, and inability of the employees to work together.
Open Whistle blowing: Individuals openly revealing their identity as they convey the information.
Anonymous Whistle blowing: Individual conveying the information conceals his/her identity

PROCEDURES TO BE FOLLOWED BEFORE WHISTLE BLOWING
- *Except* for extreme *emergencies*, always try *working through normal* organizational *channels.*
- Be *prompt* in expressing objections.
- Proceed in a tactful manner with *due consideration to the feelings* of others involved.
- As much as possible, *keep supervisors informed* of your actions, both informally and formally.
- Be accurate in observations and claims and *keep all formal records* documenting relevant events.
- *Consult* colleagues for *advice* and also to *avoid isolation.*
- *Consult the ethics committee* of your professional society before going outside the organization.
- *Consult a lawyer* regarding potential legal liabilities.

A great deal of introspection and reflection are required before WB. Motive should neither befor revenge upon fellow employee, supervisor or company nor in the hope of future gains like book contracts or speaking tours etc.

CONDITIONS TO BE SATISFIED BEFORE WHISTLE BLOWING

Richard T. De George suggests the following:

1. The *harm* that will be done by the product to the public is *serious* and considerable.
2. *The individual makes his/her concern known to his/her superiors*
3. If one does not get any proper response from immediate superiors, then one should *exhaust the channels* that are available *within the organization* including the board of directors.
4. One must have *documented evidence* that would *convince* a reasonable and impartial *observer* that one's view of the situation is correct and the company policy is wrong.
5. There must be *strong evidence* that making the information public will in fact *prevent the threatened serious harm.*

PREVENTION OF WHISTLE BLOWING

The following *actions* will *prevent/reduce* whistle blowing:

1. Giving *direct access* to higher levels of management by announcing '*open door*' policies with guarantee that *there won't be retaliation.* Instead such employees should be *rewarded for fostering ethical behavior* in the company.
2. This gives greater freedom and promotes open communication within the organization.
3. Creation of an Ethics Review Committee with *freedom to investigate complaints and make independent recommendations* to top management.
4. Top priority should be given to promote ethical conduct in the organization by top management.
5. Engineers should be allowed to discuss in confidence, their moral concerns with the ethics committee of their professional societies.
6. When there are differences on ethical issues between engineers and management, ethics committee members of the professional societies should be allowed to enter into these discussions.
7. Changes and updating in law must be explored by engineers, organizations, professional societies and government organizations on a continuous basis.

<u>4.8</u> EMPLOYEES RIGHT

- Employee rights are any rights, moral or legal, that involve the status of being an employee.

Employee rights are:
- There should be no discrimination against an employee for criticizing ethical, moral or legal policies and practices of the organization.

- The organization will not also discriminate against an employee for engaging in outside activities or for objecting to an organization directive that violates common norms of morality.
- The employee will not be deprived of any enjoyment of reasonable privacy in his/her workplace.
- No personal information about employees will be collected or kept other than what is necessary to manage the organization efficiently and to meet the legal requirements.

No employee who alleges that her/his rights have been violated will be discharged or penalized without a fair hearing by the employer organization. Some clear examples: falsifying data, avoidance on the safety of a product

Employee rights are any rights, moral or legal, that involve the status of being an employee. Employee rights are:

- [ ]   *a.* There should be no discrimination against an employee for criticizing ethical, moral or legal policies and practices of the organization.
- [ ]   *b.* The organization will not also discriminate against an employee for engaging in outside activities or for objecting to an organization directive that violates common norms of morality.
- [ ]   *c.* The employee will not be deprived of any enjoyment of reasonable privacy in his/her workplace.
- [ ]   *d.* No personal information about employees will be collected or kept other than what is necessary to manage the organization efficiently and to meet the legal requirements.
- [ ]   *e.* No employee who alleges that her/his rights have been violated will be discharged or penalized without a fair hearing by the employer organization. Some clear examples; falsifying data, avoidance on the safety of a product

<u>4.9</u> INTELLECTUAL PROPERTY RIGHTS

Intellectual Property is a term referring to a number of distinct types of creations of the mind for which property rights are recognized—and the corresponding fields of law. Under intellectual property law, owners are granted certain exclusive rights to a variety of intangible assets, such as musical, literary, and artistic works; discoveries and inventions; and words, phrases, symbols, and designs. Common types of intellectual property include copyrights, trademarks, patents, industrial design rights and trade secrets in some jurisdictions.

- Intellectual Property is a product of the human intellect that has commercial value
- Many of the rights of the ownership common to real and personal property are also common to Intellectual Property
- Intellectual Property can be bought, sold, and licensed
- Similarly it can be protected against theft and infringement by others Patent, Design & Trademark together with Copyright form TOTAL INTELLECTUALPROPERTY:

Patent

1. Derived from the Latin word,, LITTERAE PATENTES" which means,, Open Letters " or Open Documents" to confer rights and privileges.
2. A contract between an Inventor and the Government
3. An exclusive privilege monopoly right granted by the Government to the Inventor
4. Invention may be of an Industrial product or process of manufacture
5. Invention should be new, non-obvious, useful and patentable as per Patents Act
6. The right to the inventor is for limited period of time and valid only within the territorial limits of a country of grant.

Examples: a drug compound, a tool, maybe software effects

Design

- Meant for beautifying an industrial product to attract the consumer public
- Shaping, Configuration or Ornamentation of a vendible Industrial product
- Exclusive Design Rights to the originator for a limited term
- Patents & design embrace the production stage of an industrial activity

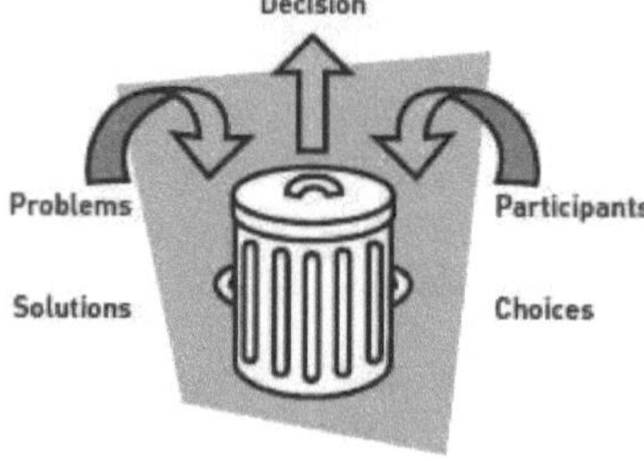

Trade Mark

- Trade Mark is a name or symbol adopted for identifying goods
- Public can identify from the Trade Mark from whom the product is emanating
- Trade Marks protection is given for an industrial product by the Government
- Examples: Channel No.5"s smell, Jacque Villeneuve's face!

COPY RIGHTS

- The right to original literary and artistic works
- Literary, written material
- Dramatic, musical or artistic works
- Films and audio-visual materials
- Sound recordings
- Computer Programmes/software
- SOME databases
- Example: Picasso"s Guernica, Microsoft code, Lord of the Rings

Need For A Patent System
a. Encourages an inventor to disclose his invention
b. Encourages R & D activities as the industries can make use of the technology, & avoids redundant research
c. Provides reasonable assurance for commercialization.
d. Provides an inducement to invest capital in the new lines of production and thus , help for technical development and upgradation.
e. One may get a very good return of income through Patent Right on the investment made in R &D.

Effect of Patent
a. A patentee gets the exclusive monopoly right against the public at large to use, sell or manufacture his patented device.
b. A patentee can enforce his monopoly right against any infringement in the court of law for suitable damages or profit of account.
c. The Government ensures full disclosure of the invention to the public for exchange of exclusive monopoly patent right to the inventor.

4.10 DISCRIMIANION

Discrimination

- Discrimination generally means preference on the grounds of sex, race, skin colour, age or religious outlook.
- In everyday speech, it has come to mean morally unjustified treatment of people on arbitrary or irrelevant grounds.
- Therefore, to call something 'Discrimination" is to condemn it.
- But when the question of justification arises, we will call it 'Preferential Treatment'.\

Discrimination is a <u>sociological term</u> referring to the <u>prejudicial</u> treatment of an individual based solely on their membership (whether voluntary or involuntary) in a certain group or category. Discrimination is the actual behavior towards members of another group. It involves excluding or restricting members of one group from opportunities that   are available to other groups. The United Nations explains: "Discriminatory behaviors take many forms, but they all involve some form of exclusion or rejection." Discriminatory laws such as redlining have existed in many countries. In some countries, controversial attempts such as racial quotas have been used to redress negative effects of discrimination.

UNIT-5
GLOBAL ISSUES

5.1 MULTINATIONAL CORPORATIONS WITH NEAT EXAMPLE

Multinational corporations conduct extensive business in more than one country. In some cases, their operations are spread so thinly around the world that their official headquarters in any one home country, as distinct from the additional host countries in which they do business, is largely incidental and essentially a matter of historical circumstance or of selection based on tax advantages.

The benefits to U.S. companies of doing business in less economically developed countries are clear: inexpensive labor, availability of natural resources, favorable tax arrangements, and fresh markets for products. The benefits to the participants in developing countries are equally clear: new jobs, jobs with higher pay and greater challenge, transfer of advanced technology, and an array of social benefits from sharing wealth. Yet moral challenges arise, accompanying business and social complications. Who loses jobs at home when manufacturing is taken—off shorel? What does the host country lose in resources, control over its own trade, and political independence? And what are the moral responsibilities of corporations and individuals operating in less economically developed countries? Here we focus on the last question. Before doing so it will be helpful to introduce the concepts of technology transfer and appropriate technology.

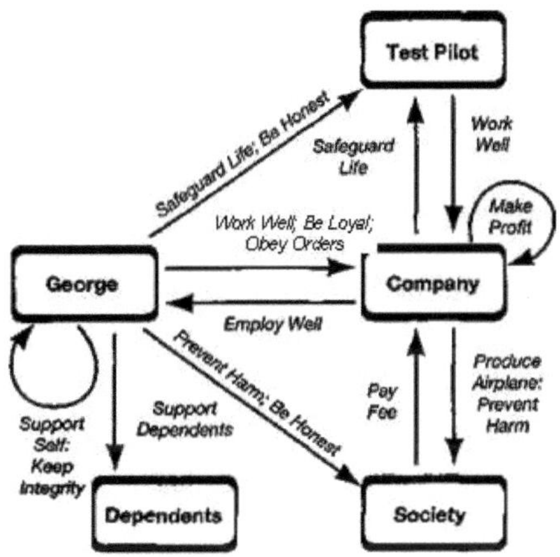

Technology Transfer and Appropriate Technology:
Technology transfer is the process of moving technology to a novel setting and implementing it there. Technology includes both hardware (machines and installations) and technique (technical, organizational, and managerial skills and procedures). A novel setting is any situation containing at least one new variable relevant to the success or failure of a given technology.

The setting may be within a country where the technology is already used elsewhere, or a foreign country, which is our present interest. A variety of agents may conduct the transfer of technology: governments, universities, private volunteer organizations (such as Engineers Without Borders), consulting firms, and multinational corporations. In most instances, the transfer of technology from a familiar to a new environment is a complex process. The technology being transferred may be one that originally evolved over a period of time and is now being introduced as a ready-made, completely new entity into a different setting. Discerning how the new setting differs from familiar contexts requires the imaginative and cautious vision of —cross-cultural social experimenters. ‖ The expression appropriate technology is widely used, but with a variety of meanings.

We use it in a generic sense to refer to identification, transfer, and implementation of the most suitable technology for a new set of conditions. Typically the conditions include social factors that go beyond routine economic and technical engineering constraints. Identifying them requires attention to an array of human values and needs that may influence how a technology affects the novel situation. Thus, in the words of Peter Heller, —appropriateness may be scrutinized in terms of scale, technical and managerial skills, materials/energy (assured availability of supply at reasonable cost), physical environment (temperature, humidity, atmosphere, salinity, water availability, etc.), capital opportunity costs (to be commensurate with benefits), but especially human values (acceptability of the end-product by the intended users in light of their institutions, traditions, beliefs, taboos, and what they consider the good life).‖5 Examples include the introduction of agricultural machines and long-distance telephones.

A country with many poor farmers can make better immediate use of small, single- or two-wheeled tractors that can serve as motorized ploughs, to pull wagons or to drive pumps, than it can of huge diesel tractors that require collectivized or agribusiness-style farming. Conversely, the same country can benefit more from the latest in wireless communication technology to spread its telephone service to more people and over long distances than it can from old-fashioned transmission by wire. Appropriate technology also implies that the technology should contribute to and not detract from sustainable development of the host country by providing for careful stewardship of its natural resources and not degrading the environment beyond its carrying capacity. Nor should technology be used to replace large numbers of individually tended small fields by large plantations to grow crops for export, leaving most of the erstwhile farmers jobless and without a source of home-grown food.

The word appropriate is vague until we answer the questions, appropriate to what, and in what way? Answering those questions immediately invokes values about human needs and environmental protection, as well as facts about situations, making it obvious that appropriate is a value-laden term. In this broader sense, the appropriate technology might sometimes be small-, intermediate-, or large-scale technology. Appropriate technology is a generic concept that applies to all attempts to emphasize wider social factors when transferring technologies. As such, it reinforces and amplifies our view of engineering as social experimentation. With these distinctions in mind, let us turn to a classic case study illustrating the complexities of engineering within multinational settings.

5.2 ENVIRONMENTAL ETHICS

Environmental ethics is the study of (*a*) moral issues concerning the environment, and (*b*) moral perspectives, beliefs, or attitudes concerning those issues. Engineers in the past are known for their negligence of environment, in their activities. It has become important now that engineers design eco-friendly tools, machines, sustainable products, processes, and projects. These are essential now to (*a*) ensure protection (safety) of environment (*b*) prevent the degradation of environment, and *(c) slowdown the exploitation of the natural resources, so that the future generation can survive.*

The American Society of Civil Engineers (ASCE) code of ethics, has specifically requires that "engineers shall hold paramount the safety, health, and welfare of the public and shall strive to comply with the principles of sustainable development in the performance of professional duties" The term sustainable development emphasizes on the investment, orientation of technology, development and functioning of organizations to meet the present needs of people and at the same time ensuring the future generations to meet their needs.

Compaq Computer Corporation (now merged with HP) was the leader, who exhibited their commitment to environmental health, through implementation of the concept of 'Design for environment' on their products, unified standards all over the world units, and giving priority to vendors with a record of environmental concern.

Engineers as experimenters have certain duties towards environmental ethics, namely:

     1. Environmental impact assessment: One major but sure and unintended effect of technology is wastage and the resulting pollution of land, water, air and even space. Study how the industry and technology affects the environment.

2. *Establish standards: Study and to fix the tolerable and actual pollution levels.*
3. *Counter measures: Study what the protective or eliminating measures are available for immediate implementation*
4. *Environmental awareness: Study on how to educate the people on environmental practices, issues, and possible remedies.*

DISASTERS

1. Plastic Waste Disposal

In our country, several crores of plastic bottles are used as containers for water and oil, and plastic bags are used to pack different materials ranging from vegetables to gold ornaments. Hardly any of these are recycled. They end up in gutters, roadsides, and agricultural fields. In all these destinations, they created havoc. The worse still is the burning of plastic materials in streets and camphor along with plastic cover in temples, since they release toxic fumes and threaten seriously the air quality. Cities and local administration have to act on this, collect and arrange for recycling through industries.

2. e-Waste Disposal

The parts of computers and electronic devices which have served its useful life present a major environmental issue for all the developing countries including India. This scrap contains highly toxic elements such as lead, cadmium, and mercury.

Even the radioactive waste will lose 89% of its toxicity after 200 years, by which time it will be no more toxic than some natural minerals in the ground. It will lose 99% of its remaining toxicity over the next 30,000 years. The toxic chemical agents such as mercury, arsenic, and cadmium retain toxicity undiminished forever.

But these scraps are illegally imported by unscrupulous agencies to salvage some commercially valuable inputs. Instead of spending and managing on the scrap, unethical organizations sell them to countries such as India. This is strictly in violation of the Basel Convention of the United Nations Environment Program, which has banned the movement of hazardous waste. A recent report of the British Environment Agency,[13] has revealed that the discarded computers, television sets, refrigerators, mobile phones, and electrical equipment's have been dispatched to India and Pakistan in large quantity, for ultimate disposal in environmentally-unacceptable ways and at great risk to the health of the labor. Even in the West, the electronic junk has been posing problems. Strong regulation including (a) pressure on industries to set up disassembling facilities, (b) ban on disposal in landfill sites, (c) legislation for recycling requirements for these junks and (d) policy incentives for eco-friendly design are essential for our country. The European Union through the Waste Electrical and Electronic Equipment (WEEE) directive has curbed thee-waste dumping by member countries and require manufacturers to implement methods to recover and recycle the components.

Indian Government expressed its concern through a technical guide on environmental management for IT Industry in December, 2004. It is yet to ratify the ban on movement of hazardous waste according to the Basel Convention. A foreign news agency exposed a few years back, the existence of a thriving e-waste disposal hub in a suburb of New Delhi, operating in appallingly dangerous conditions. Our country needs regulations to define waste, measures to stop illegal imports, and institutional structures to handle safe disposal of domestic industrial scrap.

3. Industrial Waste Disposal

There has been a lot of complaints through the media, on (a) against the Sterlite Copper Smelting Plantin Thuthukkudi (1997) against its pollution, and (b) when Indian companies imported the discarded French Warship Clemenceau for disposal, the poisonous asbestos compounds were expected to pollute the atmosphere besides exposing the labor to a great risk, during the disposal. The government did not act immediately. Fortunately for Indians, the French Government intervened and withdrew the ship, and the serious threat was averted!

4. Depletion of Ozone Layer

The ozone layer protects the entire planet from the ill-effects of ultraviolet radiation and is vital for all living organisms in this world. But it is eaten away by the Chloro-fluro-carbons (CFC) such as freon emanating from the refrigerators, air conditioners, and aerosol can spray. This has caused also skin cancer to sun-bathers in the Western countries. Further NO and NO2 gases were also found to react with the ozone. Apart from engineers, the organizations, laws of the country and local administration and market mechanisms are required to take up concerted efforts to protect the environment.

5. Global Warming

Over the past 30 years, the Earth has warmed by 0.6 °C. Over the last 100 years, it has warmed by 0.8 °C. It is likely to push up temperature by 3°C by 2100, according to NASA's studies. The U.S. administration has accepted the reality of global climate change, which has been associated with stronger hurricanes, severed roughts, intense heat waves and the melting of polar ice. Greenhouse gases, notably carbon dioxide emitted by motor vehicles and coal-fired power plants, trap heat like the glass walls of a greenhouse, cause the Earth to warm up. Delegates from the six countries — Australia, China, India, Japan, South Korea and US metin California in April 2006 for the first working session of the Asia Pacific Partnership on Clean Development and Climate. These six countries account for about half of the world's emissions of climate-heating greenhouse gases. Only one of the six, Japan, is committed to reducing greenhouse gas emissions by at least 5.2 per cent below 1990 levels by 2012 under the Kyoto Agreement.

About 190 nations met in Germany in the middle of May 2006 and tried to bridge vast policy gaps between the United States and its main allies over how to combat climate change amid growing evidence that the world is warming that could wreak havoc by stoking more droughts, heatwaves, floods, more powerful storms and raise global sea levels by almost a meter by 2100.

6. Acid Rain

Large emissions of Sulphur oxides and nitrous oxides are being released in to the air from the thermal power stations using the fossil fuels, and several processing industries. These gases form compounds with water in the air and precipitates as rain or snow on to the earth. The acid rain in some parts of the world has caused sufficient damage to the fertility of the land and to the human beings.

In addition to global warming, environmental challenges confront us at every turn, including myriad forms of pollution, human-population growth, extinction of species, destruction of ecosystems, depletion of natural resources, and nuclear waste. Today there is a wide consensus that we need concerted environmental responses that combine economic realism with ecological

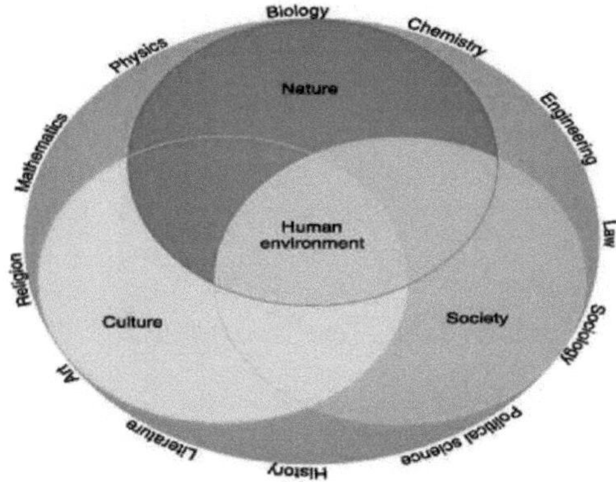

Engineering ecology and economics:
Two powerful metaphors have dominated thinking about the environment: the invisible hand and the tragedy of the commons. Both metaphors are used to highlight unintentional impacts of the marketplace on the environment, but one is optimistic and the other is cautionary about those impacts. Each contains a large part of the truth, and they need to be reconciled and balanced. The first metaphor was set forth by Adam Smith in 1776 in The Wealth of Nations, the founding text of modern economics. Smith conceived of an invisible (and divine) hand governing the Market place in a seemingly paradoxical manner. According to Smith, businesspersons think only of their own self-interest; It is not from the benevolence of the butcher, the brewer, or the baker, that we expect our dinner, but from the irregard to their own interest. Yet, although— he intends only his own gain, Ihe is—led by an invisible hand to promote an end which was no part of his intention. By pursuing his own interest, he frequently promotes that of the society more effectually than when he really intends to promote it. I have never known much good done by those who affected to trade for the public good.

In fact, professionals and many business persons do profess to—trade for the public good, ‖ claiming a commitment to hold paramount the safety, health, and welfare of the public. Although they are predominantly motivated by self-interest, they also have genuine moral concern for others.3 Nevertheless, Smith's metaphor of the invisible hand contains a large element of truth. By pursuing self-interest, the business person, as entrepreneur, creates new companies that provide goods and services for consumers. Moreover, competition pressures corporations to continually improve the quality of their products and to lower prices, again benefiting consumers. In addition, new jobs are created for employees and suppliers, and the wealth generated benefits the wider community through consumerism, taxes, and philanthropy.

Despite its large element of truth, the invisible hand metaphor does not adequately take account of damage to the environment. Writing in the eighteenth century, with its seemingly infinite natural resources, Adam Smith could not have foreseen the cumulative impact of expanding populations, unregulated capitalism, and market —externalities‖—that is, economic impacts not included in the cost of products. Regarding the environment, most of these are negative externalities—pollution, destruction of natural habitats, depletion of shared resources, and other unintended and often unappreciated damage to —common ‖resources. This damage is the topic of the second metaphor, which is rooted in Aristotle's observation that we tend to be thoughtless about things we do no town individually and which seem to be in unlimited supply. William Foster Lloyd was also an astute observer of this phenomenon.

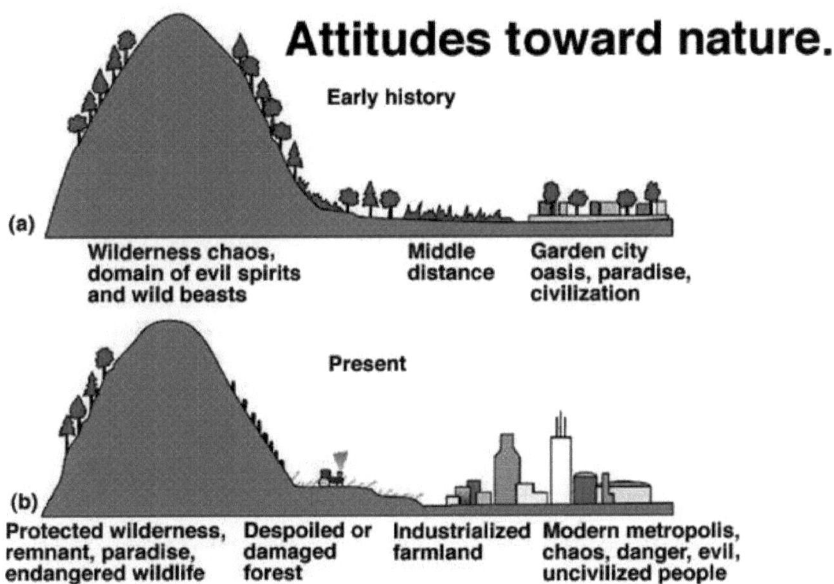

In1833hedescribedwhat the ecologist Garrett Hardin would later call —the tragedy of the commons. Lloyd observed that cattle in the common pasture of a village were more stunted than those kept on private land. The common fields were themselves more worn than private pastures. His explanation began with the premise that individual farmers are understandably motivated by self-interest to enlarge their common-pasture herd by one or two cows, especially given that each act taken by itself does negligible damage. Yet, when all the farmers behave this way, in the absence of laws constraining them, the result is the tragedy of overgrazing that harms everyone.

5.3 HUMAN-CENTERED ETHICS

Human-centered, or anthropocentric, environmental ethics focuses exclusively on the benefits of the natural environment to humans and the threats to human beings presented by the destruction of nature. In their classic formulations, all of them assume that, among the creatures on earth, only human beings have inherent moral worth and hence deserve to be taken into account in making moral decisions concerning the environment (or anything else). Other creatures and eco systems have at most —instrumental value—as means to promoting human interests.
Utilitarian's enjoin us to maximize good consequences for human beings. In developing an environmental ethic, the relevant goods consist of human interests and goods linked to nature. Many of those pleasures and interests concern engineered products made from natural resources.

In addition, we have aesthetic interests, as in the beauty of plants, waterfalls, and mountain ranges, and recreational interests, as in hiking and backpacking in wilderness areas. We have scientific interests, especially in the study of— natural labs of ecological preserves, such as the rain forests. And most basic, we have survival interests, which are linked directly to conserving resources and preserving the natural environment.

The typical argument of rights ethics is that the basic rights to life and to liberty entail a right to a livable environment. The right to a livable environment did not generally enter into people's thinking until the end of the twentieth century, at the time when pollution and resource depletion reached alarming proportions. Nevertheless, it is directly implied by the rights to life and liberty, given that these basic rights cannot be exercised without a supportive natural environment. A right to a livable environment is implied by rights to life and to liberty, and it —imposes upon everyone a correlative moral obligation to respect.

In duty ethics, which makes duties rather than rights fundamental, respect for human life implies far greater concern for nature than has been traditionally recognized. Kant believed that we owe duties only to rational beings, which in his view excluded all non-human animals, although of course he did not have access to recent scientific studies showing striking parallels between humans and other primates. Nevertheless, he condemned callousness and cruelty toward conscious animals because he saw the danger that such attitudes would foster in human treatment of persons. In any case, a duty-centered ethics would emphasize the need for conserving the environment because doing so is implied by respect for human beings who depend on it for their very existence.

Finally, virtue ethics draws attention to such virtues as prudence, humility, appreciation of beauty, and gratitude toward the natural world that makes life possible, and also the virtue of stewardship over resources that are needed for further generations. Thomas E. Hill, Jr., offers an anecdote: —A wealthy eccentric bought a house in a neighborhood I know. The house was surrounded by a beautiful display of grass, plants, and flowers, and it was shaded by a huge old avocado tree. But the grass required cutting, the flowers needed tending, and the man wanted more sun. So he cut the whole lot down and covered the yard with asphalt. The man's attitudes, suggests Hill, are comparable to the callousness shown in strip mining, the cutting of redwood forests, and other destruction of ecosystems with blinkered visions of usefulness. All these human-centered ethics permit and indeed require a long-term view of conserving the environment, especially because the human beings who have inherent worth will include future generations. Not everything of importance within a human-centered ethics fits neatly into cost-benefit analyses with limited time horizons; much must be accounted for by means of constraints or limits that cannot necessarily be assigned dollar signs.

Yet, some have argued that all versions of human-centered ethics are flawed and that we should widen the circle of things that have inherent worth, that is, value in themselves, independent of human desires and appraisals. Especially since 1979, when the journal Environmental Ethics was founded, philosophers have explored a wide range of nature- centered ethics that, for example, affirm the inherent worth of all conscious animals, of all living organisms, or of ecosystems. Let us consider each of these approaches.

Computers have become the technological backbone of society. Their degree of complexity, range of applications, and sheer numbers continue to increase. Through telecommunication networks they span the globe. Yet electronic computers are still only a Few decades old, and it is difficult to fore see all the moral issues that will eventually surround them. The present state of computers is sometimes compared to that of the automobile in the early part of this century. At that time the impact of cars on work and leisure patterns, pollution, energy consumption, and sexual mores was largely unimagined. If anything, it is more difficult to envisage the eventual impact of computers because they are not limited to any one primary area of use as is a car's function in transportation.

It is already clear, however, that computers raise a host of difficult moral issues, many of them connected with basic moral concerns such as free speech, privacy, respect for property, informed consent, and harm. To evaluate and deal with these issues, a new area of applied ethics called computer ethics has sprung up. Computer ethics has special importance for the new groups of professionals emerging with computer technology, for example, designers of computers, programmers, systems analysts, and operators. To the extent that engineers design, manufacture, and apply computers, computer ethics is a branch of engineering ethics. But the many professionals who use and control computers share the responsibility for their applications.

Some of the issues in computer ethics concern shifts in power relationships resulting from the new capacities of computers. Other issues concern property, and still others are about invasions of privacy. All these issues may involve —computer abusel: unethical or illegal conduct in which computers play a central role (whether as instruments or objects).

The Internet and Free Speech:
The Internet has magnified all issues in computer ethics. The most powerful communication technology ever developed, and a technology used daily by hundreds of millions of people, the Internet gained widespread use only during the 1990s. Its modest beginning, or forerunner, came from a simple idea of J. C. R. Licklider.2 Lick lider was a psychologist who had wide interests in the newly emerging computer technology. In 1960he conceived of a human- computer symbiosis in which the powers of humans and computers were mutually enhancing.3 The breadth of his vision, together with his administrative skills, led to his appointment a few years later as the director of the Advanced Research Projects Agency (ARPA) of the U.S. Department of Defense. He quickly saw that the variety of computer-involved military projects was becoming a Tower of Babel, and he wrote a revolutionary memo calling for a move toward a unified communication system. In 1969, ARPA funded projects in universities and corporations that created an ARPA network, or ARPANET.

In the 1980s, some universities developed their own communications networks, and their eventual merging with ARPANET became the Internet, which is now a global network of networks, initially using the infrastructure of the telephone system and now carried by many telecommunication systems by wire, fibre, or wireless systems. The World Wide Web (Web), which is a service run on the Internet, emerged from the Hypertext Mark-up Language and transfer protocol developed at the European particle physics lab and is used in a multimedia format of text, pictures, sound, and video. During the early 1990s, the Web was opened to business, e-mail, and other uses that continue to expand. It is now clear to all that the Internet provides a wellspring of new ways to be in contact with other people and with sources of information. It has also created greater convenience in ordering consumer items, paying bills, and trading stocks and bonds. Like other major —social experiments, it also has raised a host of new issues. One set of issues centres on free speech including control of obscene forms of pornography, hate speech, spam (unwanted commercial speech), and libel. In a wide sense, pornography is sexually explicit material intended primarily for sexual purposes (as distinct, say, from medical education).

Obscene pornography is pornography that is immoral or illegal in many countries, and is not protected in the United States by the First Amendment rights to free speech. U.S. laws define obscenity as sexually explicit materials that appeal to sexual interests, lack serious literary, artistic, scientific, or other value, and are offensive to reasonable persons as judged by a community 's standards. Needless to say, there is considerable disagreement about what this means, and the definition is relative to communities that might have differing standards.
At the same time, there is wide agreement that child pornography and extremely violent and degrading portrayals of women are obscene, and most local communities have attempted to control them. The Internet has made such control extremely difficult, as images and texts can be transmitted easily from international sources to a child's home computer. There are now hundreds of thousands of pornographic Websites, with hundreds more created each day, many of which contain obscene material. Hate speech, unlike obscenity, is not forbidden constitutionally. Not surprisingly, then, the Internet has become a powerful resource for racist and anti-Semitic groups to spread their messages. Those messages were heard, for example, by Eric Harris and Dylan Klebold, who massacred their fellow students at Columbine High School in 1999. And there is no question that this most powerful medium makes it much easier for hate groups to organize and expand.

1 TYPES OF ISSUES
Different types of problems are found in computer ethics.
1. Computer as the Instrument of Unethical Acts
  (a) The usage of computer replaces the job positions. This has been overcome to a large extent by readjusting work assignments, and training everyone on computer applications such as word processing, editing, and graphics.
  (b) Breaking privacy. Information or data of the individuals accessed or erased or the ownership changed.
  (c) Defraud a bank or a client, by accessing and withdrawing money from other's bank account.
2. Computer as the Object of Unethical Act
The data are accessed and deleted or changed.
  (a) *Hacking*: The software is stolen or information is accessed from other computers. This may cause financial loss to the business or violation of privacy rights of the

individuals or business. In case of defense information being hacked, this may endanger the security of the nation.

(b) *Spreading virus*: Through mail or otherwise, other computers are accessed and the files are erased or contents changed altogether. 'Trojan horses' are implanted to distort the messages and files beyond recovery. This again causes financial loss or mental torture to the individuals. Some hackers feel that they have justified their right of free information or they do it for fun. However, these acts are certainly unethical.

(c) *Health hazard*: The computers pose threat during their use as well as during disposal. These are discussed in # 5.3.2 and # 5.2.1, respectively, in detail.

3. Problems Related to the Autonomous Nature of Computer

(a) *Security risk*: Recently the Tokyo Stock Exchange faced a major embarrassment. A seemingly casual mistake by a junior trader of a large security house led to huge losses including that of reputation. The order through the exchange's trading system was to sell one share for 600,000 *Yen*. Instead, the trader keyed in a sale order for 600,000 shares at the rate of one *Yen* each. Naturally the shares on offer at the ridiculously low price were lapped up. And only a few buyers agreed to reverse the deal! The loss to the securities firm was said to be

Huge, running into several hundred thousands. More important to note, such an obvious mistake could not be corrected by some of the advanced technology available. For advanced countries like Japan who have imbibed the latest technology, this would be a new kind of learningexperience.[12]

(b) *Loss of human lives*: Risk and loss of human lives lost by computer, in the operational control of military weapons. There is a dangerous instability in automated defense system. An unexpected error in the software or hardware or a conflict during interfacing between the two, may trigger a serious attack and cause irreparable human loss before the error is traced. The Chinese embassy was bombed by U.S. military in Iraq a few years back, but enquiries revealed that the building was shown in a previous map as the building where in surgent stayed.

(c) In flexible manufacturing systems, the autonomous computer is beneficial in obtaining continuous monitoring and automatic control.

Various issues related to computer ethics are discussed as follows:

COMPUTERS IN WORKPLACE

The ethical problems initiated by computers in the workplace are:

1. Elimination of routine and manual jobs. This leads to unemployment, but the creation of skilled and IT- enabled service jobs are more advantageous for the people. Initially this may require some upgradation of their skills and knowledge, but a formal training will set this problem right. For example, in place of a typist, we have a programmer or an accountant.

2. *Health and safety*: The ill-effects due to electromagnetic radiation, especially on women and pregnant employees, mental stress, wrist problem known as *Carpel Tunnel Syndrome*, and backpain due to poor ergonomic seating designs, and eye strain due to

poor lighting and flickers in the display and long exposure, have been reported worldwide. Over a period of long exposure, these are expected to affect the health and safety of the people. The computer designers should take care of these aspects and management should monitor the health and safety of the computer personnel.

3. *Computer failure*: Failure in computers may be due to errors in the hardware or software. Hardware errors are rare and they can be solved easily and quickly. But software errors are very serious as they can stop the entire network. Testing and quality systems for software have gained relevance and importance in the recent past, to avoid or minimize these errors.

PROPERTY ISSUES

The property issues concerned with the computers are:

1. Computers have been used to extort money through anonymous telephone calls.
2. Computers are used to cheat and steal by current as well as previous employees.
3. Cheating of and stealing from the customers and clients.
4. Violation of contracts on computer sales and services.
5. Conspiracy as a group, especially with the internet, to defraud the gullible, stealing the identity and to forge documents.
6. Violation of property rights: Is the software a property? The software could be either a Program (an algorithm, indicating the steps in solving a problem) or a Source code (the algorithm in a general computer language such as FORTAN, C and COBOL oran Object code (to translate the source code into the machine language). How do we apply the concept of property here? This demands a framework for ethical judgments.

7. Property is what the laws permits and defines as can be owned, exchanged, and used. The computer hardware (product) is protected by patents. The software (idea, expression) is protected by copyrights and trade secrets. But algorithms cannot be copyrighted, because the mathematical formulas can be discovered but not owned. The object codes which are not intelligible to human beings cannot be copyrighted.
8. Thus, we see that reproducing multiple copies from one copy of (licensed) software and distribution or sales are crimes. The open-source concepts have, to a great extent, liberalized and promoted the use of computer programs for the betterment of society.

COMPUTER CRIME

The ethical features involved in computer crime are:

1. ***Physical Security:*** The computers are to be protected against theft, fire, and physical damage. This can be achieved by proper insurance on the assets.
2. ***Logical security:*** The aspects related are (*a*) the privacy of the individuals or organizations, (*b*) confidentiality, (*c*) integrity, to ensure that the modification of data or program are done only by the authorized persons, (*d*) uninterrupted service. This is achieved by installing appropriate uninterrupted power supply or back-up provisions, and (*e*) protection against hacking that causes dislocation or distortion. Licensed anti-virus packages and firewalls are used by all computer users to ensure this protection.

Passwords and data encryption have been incorporated in the computer software as security measures. But these have also been attacked and bye-passed. But this problem is not been solved completely.

Major weaknesses in this direction are: (*a*) the difficulty in tracing the evidence involved and (*b*) absence of stringent punishment against the crime. The origin of a threat to the Central Government posted from an obscure browsing center, remained unsolved for quite a long time. Many times, such crimes have been traced, but there are no clear *cyber laws* to punish and deter the criminals.

PRIVACY AND ANONYMITY

The data transmission and accessibility have improved tremendously by using the computers, but the right to privacy has been threatened to a great extent. Some issues concerned with the privacy are listed hereunder:

1. ***Records of Evidence:*** Service records or criminal records and the details of people can be stored and accessed to prove the innocence or guilty. Records on psychiatric treatment by medical practitioners or hospital, or records of membership of organizations may sometime embarrass the persons in later years.

2. ***Hacking:*** There are computer enthusiasts who willfully or for fun, plant virus or "Trojan horses" that may fill the disc space, falsify information, erase files, and even harm the hardware. They breakdown the functioning of computers and can be treated as violation of property rights. Some hackers opine that the information should be freely available for everybody. It is prudent that the right to individual privacy in limiting the access to the information on one self, should not be violated. Further any unauthorized use of personal information (which is a property), is to be considered as theft. Besides the individual privacy, the national security, and freedom within the economy are to be respected. The proprietary information and data of the organizations are to be protected so that they can pursue the goals without hindrance.

3. ***Legal Response:*** In the Indian scene, the Right to Information Act 2005 [14] provides the right to the citizens to secure access to information *under the control of public authorities*, including the departments of the central government, state governments, government bodies, public sector companies and public sector banks, to promote transparency and
accountability of public authorities.

4. **Right to information**: Under the Act, section 2 (*j*), the right to information includes the right to (1) Inspect works, documents, records, (2) take notes, extracts or certified copies of documents or records, (3) take certified samples of material, and (4) obtain information in the form of printouts, diskettes, floppies, tapes, video cassettes or in any other electronic mode.

55 INVOLMENT IN WEAPONS WORK

Historically, a quick death in battle by sword was considered acceptable, whereas the use of remote weapons (from bow and arrow to firearms) was frequently decried as cowardly, devoid of valour, and tantamount to plain murder.16 As modern weapons of war progressed through catapults, cannons, machineguns, and bombs released from air planes and missiles to reach further and further, the soldiers firing them were less likely to see the individual human beings—soldiers as well as civilians—they had as their general target. The continuing automation of the battle scene tends to conceal the horrors of war and thus makes military activity seem less threatening and high- tech wars more appealing. How might the men and women who design weapons, manufacture them, and use them feel about their work? For some engineers, involvement in weapons development conflicts with personal conscience; for others, it is an expression of conscientious participation in national defense. The following cases illustrate the kinds of moral issues involved in deciding whether to engage in military work.

1. Bob's employer manufactures antipersonnel bombs. By clustering 665 guava-size bomb lets and letting them explode above ground, an area covering the equivalent of 10 football fields is subjected to a shower of sharp fragments. Alternatively, the bombs can be timed to explode hours apart after delivery. Originally the fragments were made of steel, and thus they were often removable with magnets; now plastic materials are sometimes used, making the treatment of wounds, including the location and removal of the fragments, more time-consuming for the surgeon. Recently another innovation was introduced: By coating the bomb lets with phosphorus, the fragments could inflict internal burns as well. Thus, the antipersonnel bomb does its job quite well without necessarily killing in that it ties up much of the enemy's resources just in treating the wounded who have survived. Bob himself does not handle the bombs in any way, but as an industrial engineer he enables the factory to run efficiently. He does not like to be involved in making weapons, but then he tells himself that someone has to produce them. If he does not do his job, someone else will, so nothing would change. Furthermore, with the cost of living being what it is, he owes his family a steady income.

2. Mary is a chemical engineer. A promotion has gotten her into napalm manufacturing. She knows it is nasty stuff, having heard that the Nobel laureate, Professor Wald of Harvard University, was said to have be rated the chemical industry for producing this— most brutal and destructive weapon that has ever been created. She saw a scary old photograph from the Vietnam War period, depicting a badly burned peasant girl running from a village inflames. But the locals were said to take forever in leaving a fighting zone and then there were complaints about them being hurt or killed. She abhors war like most human beings, but she feels that the government knows more than she does about international dangers and that the present use of napalm by U.S. forces in Iraq may be unavoidable. Regarding her own future, Mary knows that if she continues to do well on her job she will be promoted, and one of these days she may well be in the position to steer the company into the production of peaceful products. Will Mary use a higher position in the way she hopes to do, or will she instead wait until she becomes the CEO? Ron is a specialist in missile control and guidance. He is proud to be able to help his country through his efforts in the defense industry, especially as part of the —war on terrorism. The missiles he works on will carry single or multiple warheads with the kind of dreadful firepower which, in his estimation, has kept any potential enemy in check since 1945. At least there has not been another world war—the result of mutual deterrence, he believes.

3. Marco's foremost love is physical electronics. He works in one of the finest laser laboratories. Some of his colleagues do exciting research in particle beams. That the laboratory is interested in developing something a into the— death rayǁ described by science fiction writers of his you this of secondary importance. More bothersome is the secrecy that prevents him from freely exchanging ideas with experts across the world. But why change jobs if he will never find facilities like those he has now?

4. Joanne is electronics engineer whose work assignment includes avionics for fighter planes that are mostly sold abroad. She has no qualms about such planes going to what she considers friendly countries, but she draws the line at their sale to potentially hostile nations. Joanne realizes that she has no leverage within the company, so she occasionally alerts journalist friends with news she feels all citizens should have. —Let the voters direct the country at election timeǁ— that is her motto.

5. Ted's background and advanced degrees in engineering physics gave him a ready entry into nuclear bomb development. As a well-informed citizen he is seriously concerned with the dangers of the ever-growing nuclear arsenal. He is also aware of the possibilities of an accidental nuclear exchange. In the mean-time he is working hard to reduce the risk of accidents such as the 32—broken arrows ǁ (incidents when missile launchings may have occurred erroneously) that had been reported by the Pentagon during the height of the Cold War, or the many others than the knows have occurred worldwide. Ted continues in his work because he believes that only specialists, with firsthand experience of what modern weapons can do, can eventually turn around the suicidal trend represented by their development. Who else can engage in meaningful arms control negotiations?

WEAPONSDEVELOPMENT

Military activities including the world wars have stimulated the growth of technology. The growth of Internet amply illustrates this fact. The development of warfare and the involvement of engineers bring out many ethical issues concerned with engineers, such as the issue of integrity in experiments as well as expenditure in defense research and development, issue of personal commitment and conscience, and the issues of social justice and social health.

Engineers involve in weapons development because of the following reasons:
1. It gives one job with high salary.
2. One takes pride and honor in participating in the activities towards the defense of the nation (patriotic fervor).
3. One believes the he fights a war on terrorism and thereby contribute to peace and stability of the country. Ironically, the wars have never won peace, only peace can win peace!
4. By research and development, the engineer is reducing or eliminating the risk from enemy weapons, and saving one's country from disaster.
5. By building-up arsenals and show of force, a country can force the rogue country, towards regulation. Engineers can participate effectively in arms control negotiations for surrender or peace, e.g., bombing of Nagasaki and Hiroshima led to surrender by the Japanese in 1945.

Many engineers had to fight and convince their personal conscience. The scene such as that of a Vietnamese village girl running wild with burns on the body and horror in the face and curse in her mind has moved some engineers away from their jobs.

<u>56</u> ENGINEERS AS MANAGERS

CHARACTERISTICS
The characteristics of engineers as managers are:
1. Promote an ethical climate, through framing organization policies, responsibilities and by personal attitudes and obligations.
2. Resolving conflicts, by evolving priority, developing mutual understanding, generating various alternative solutions to problems.
3. Social responsibility to stakeholders, customers and employers. They act to develop wealth as well as the welfare of the society. Ethicists project the view that the manager's responsibility is only to increase the profit of the organization, and only the engineers have the responsibility to protect the safety, health, and welfare of the public. But managers have the ethical responsibility to produce safe and good products (or useful service), while showing respect for the human beings who include the employees, customers and the public. Hence, the objective for the managers and engineers is to produce valuable products that are also profitable.

MANAGING CONFLICTS
In solving conflicts, force should not be resorted. In fact, the conflict situations should be tolerated, understood, and resolved by participation by all the concerned. The conflicts in case of project managers arise in the following manners:
(a) Conflicts based on schedules: This happens because of various levels of execution, priority and limitations of each level.
(b) Conflicts arising out of fixing the priority to different projects or departments. This is to be arrived at from the end requirements and it may change from time to time.
(c) Conflict based on the availability of personnel.
(d) Conflict over technical, economic, and time factors such as cost, time, and performance level.
(e) Conflict arising in administration such as authority, responsibility, accountability, and logistics required.
(f) Conflicts of personality, human psychology and ego problems.
(g) Conflict over expenditure and its deviations.

Most of the conflicts can be resolved by following the principles listed here:

1. People

Separate people from the problem. It implies that the views of all concerned should be obtained. The questions such as what, why, and when the error was committed is more important than to know who committed it. This impersonal approach will lead to not only early solution but also others will be prevented from committing errors.

2. Interests

Focus must be only on interest i.e., the ethical attitudes or motives and not on the positions (i.e., stated views). A supplier may require commission larger than usual prevailing rate for an agricultural product.

But the past analysis may tell us that the material is not cultivated regularly and the monsoon poses some additional risk towards the supply. Mutual interests must be respected to a maximum level. What is right is more important than who is right!

3. Options

Generate various options as solutions to the problem. This helps a manager to try the next best solution should the first one fails. Decision on alternate solutions can be taken more easily and without loss of time.

4. Evaluation

The evaluation of the results should be based on some specified objectives such as efficiency, quality, and customer satisfaction. More important is that the means, not only the goals, should be ethical.

5.7 CONSULTING ENGINEERS

The consulting engineers work in private. There is no salary from the employers. But they charge fees from the sponsor and they have more freedom to decide on their projects. Still they have no absolute freedom, because they need to earn for their living. The consulting engineers have ethical responsibilities different from the salaried engineers, as follows:

1. Advertising

The consulting engineers are directly responsible for advertising their services, even if they employ other consultants to assist them. But in many organizations, this responsibility is with the advertising executives and the personnel department.

They are allowed to advertise but to avoid deceptive ones. Deceptive advertising such as the following are prohibited:

- (a) By white lies.
- (b) Half-truth, e.g., a product has actually been tested as prototype, but it was claimed to have been already introduced in the market. An architect shows the photograph of the completed building with flowering trees around but actually the foundation of the building has been completed and there is no real garden.
- (c) Exaggerated claims. The consultant might have played a small role in a well-known project. But they could claim to have played a major role.
- (d) Making false suggestions. The reduction in cost might have been achieved along with the reduction in strength, but the strength details are hidden.
- (e) Through vague wordings or slogans.

2. Competitive Bidding

It means offering a price, and get something in return for the service offered. The organizations have a pool of engineers. The expertise can be shared and the bidding is made more realistic. But the individual consultants have to develop creative designs and build their reputation steadily and carefully, over a period of time. The clients will have to choose between the reputed organizations and proven qualifications of the company and the expertise of the consultants. Although competent, the younger consultants are thus slightly at a disadvantage.

3. Contingency Fee

This is the fee or commission paid to the consultant, when one is successful in saving the expenses for the client. A sense of honesty and fairness is required in fixing this fee. The NSPE Code III 6 (*a*) says that the engineers shall not propose or accept a commission on a contingent basis where their judgment may be compromised. The fee may be either as an agreed amount or a fixed percentage of the savings realized. But in the contingency fee-agreements, the judgment of the consultant may be biased. The consultant may be tempted to specify inferior materials or design methods to cut the construction cost. This fee may motivate the consultants to effect saving in the costs to the clients, through reasonably moral and technological means.

4. Safety and Client's Needs

The greater freedom for the consulting engineers in decision making on safety aspects, and difficulties concerning truthfulness are the matters to be given attention. For example, in design-only projects, the consulting engineers may design something and have no role in the construction. Sometimes, difficulties may crop-up during construction due to non-availability of suitable materials, some shortcuts in construction, and lack of necessary and adequate supervision and inspection. Properly-trained supervision is needed, but may not happen, unless it is provided. Further, the contractor may not understand and/or be willing to modify the original design to serve the clients best.

A few on-site inspections by the consulting engineers will expose the deficiency in execution and save the workers, the public, and the environment that may be exposed to risk upon completion of the project.

The NSPE codes on the advertisement by consultants provide some specific regulations. The following are the activities prohibited in advertisement by consultant:

1. The use of statement containing misrepresentation or omission of a necessary fact.
2. Statement intended or likely to create an unjustified expectation.
3. Statement containing prediction of future (probable)success.
4. Statement intended or likely to attract clients, by the use of slogans or sensational language format.

5.8 ENGINEERS AS EXPERT WITNESS AND ADVISORS

Frequently engineers are required to act as consultants and provide expert opinion and views in many legal cases of the past events. They are required to explain the causes of accidents, malfunctions and other technological behavior of structures, machines, and instruments, e.g., personal injury while using an instrument, defective product, traffic accident, structure or building collapse, and damage to the property, are some of the cases where testimonies are needed. The focus is on the past.

Eye-witness	*Expert-witness*
1. Eye witness gives evidence on only	1. Gives expert view on the facts in their area

	of
what has been seen or heard actually (perceived facts)	their expertise 2. Interprets the facts, in term of the cause and effect relationship 3. Comments on the view of the opposite side 4. Reports on the professional standards, especially on the precautions when the product is made or the service is provided

The engineers, who act as expert-witnesses, are likely to abuse their positions in the following manners:

1. Hired Guns
Mostly lawyers hire engineers to serve the interest of their clients. Lawyers are permitted and required to project the case in a way favorable to their clients. But the engineers have obligations to thoroughly examine the events and demonstrate their professional integrity to testify only the truth in the court. They do not serve the clients of the lawyers directly. The hired guns forward white lies and distortions, as demanded by the lawyers. They even withhold the information or shade the fact, to favor their clients.

2. Money Bias
Consultants may be influenced or prejudiced for monitory considerations, gain reputation and make a fortune.

3. Ego Bias
The assumption that the own- side is innocent and the other side is guilty, is responsible for this behavior. An inordinate desire to serve one's client and get name and fame is another reason for this bias.

4. Sympathy Bias
Sympathy for the victim on the opposite side may upset the testimony. The integrity of the consultants will keep these biases away from the justice. The court also must obtain the balanced view of both sides, by examining the expert witnesses of lawyers on both sides, to remove a probable bias.

Duties
1. The expert- witness is required to exhibit the responsibility of *confidentiality* just as they do in the consulting roles. They cannot divulge the findings of the investigation to the opposite side, unless it is required by the court of law.
2. More important is that as witness they are *not required to volunteer* evidence favorable to the opponent. They must answer questions truthfully, need note labor ate, and remain neutral until the details are asked for further.
3. They should be *objective* to discover the truth and communicate them honestly.

4. The stand of the experts depends on the *shared understanding* created within the society. The legal system should be respected and at the same time, they should act in conformance with the professional standards as obtained from the code of ethics.

5. The experts should earnestly be *impartial* in identifying and interpreting the observed data, recorded data, and the industrial standards. They should not distort the truth, even under pressure. Although they are hired by the lawyers, they do not serve the lawyers or their clients. They serve the justice. Many a time, their objective judgments will help the lawyer to put up the best defense for their clients.

ENGINEERS AS ADVISORS IN PLANNING AND POLICY MAKING

Advisors

The engineers are required to give their view on the future such as in planning, policy-making, which involves the technology. For example, should India expand nuclear power options or support traditional energy sources such as fossil fuels or alternative forms like solar and wind energy? In the recent past, this topic has created lot of fireworks, in the national media.

Various issues and requirements for engineers who act as advisors are:

1. Objectivity

The engineers should study the cost and benefits of all possible alternative means in objective manner, within the specified conditions and assumptions.

2. Study All Aspects

They have to study the economic viability (effectiveness), technical feasibility (efficiency), operational feasibility (skills) and social acceptability, which include environmental and ethical aspects, before formulating the policy.

3. Values

Engineers have to posses the qualities, such as (*a*) honesty, (*b*) competence (skills and expertise), (*c*) diligence (careful and alert) (*d*) loyalty in serving the interests of the clients and maintaining confidentiality, and (*e*) public trust, and respect for the common good, rather than serving only the interests of the clients or the political interests.

4. Technical Complexity

The arbitrary, unrealistic, and controversial assumptions made during the future planning that are overlooked or not verified, will lead to moral complexity. The study on future is full of uncertainties than the investigations on the past events. On the study of energy options, for example, assumptions on population increase, life style, urbanization, availability of local fossil resources, projected costs of generating alternative forms of energy, world political scenario, world military tensions and pressures from world organizations such as World Trade Organization (W.T.O.) and European Union (EU) may increase the complexity in judgment on future.

5. National Security

The proposed options should be aimed to strengthen the economy and security of the nation, besides safe guarding the natural resources and the environment from exploitation and degradation.

For the advisors on policy making or planning, a shared understanding on balancing the conflicting responsibilities, both to the clients and to the public, can be affected by the following roles or models:

1. Hired Gun

The prime obligation is shown to the clients. The data and facts favorable to the clients are highlighted, and unfavorable aspects are hidden or treated as insignificant. The minimal level of interest is shown for public welfare.

2. Value-neutral Analysts

This assumes an impartial engineer. They exhibit conscientious decisions, impartiality i.e., without bias, fear or favor, and absence of advocacy.

3. Value-guided Advocates

The consulting engineers remain honest (frank in stating all there levant facts and truthful in interpretation of the facts) and autonomous (independent) in judgement and show paramount importance to the public (as different from the hired guns).

<u>59</u> HONESTY

Honesty means expressing your true feelings. To be able to be emotionally honest we must first be emotionally aware. This emotional awareness is related to our emotional intelligence. Itis our emotional intelligence, which gives us the ability to accurately identify our feelings.

Emotional intelligence may also give us the ability to decide when it is in our best interest to be emotionally honest by sharing our real feelings. We would be better off individually and as a society if we would be more honest. If we are more honest with ourselves, we will get to know our —true selves‖ on a deeper level. This could help us become more self-accepting. It could also help us make better choices about how to spend out time and who to spend it with.

If we are honest with other, it may encourage them to be more emotionally honest. When we are emotionally honest, we are more likely not to be asked or pressured to do things which we do not want to do. We will also find out sooner who respects our feelings.

How society discourages honesty?

It takes awareness, self-confidence, even courage to be emotionally honest. This is because, in many ways, society teaches us to ignore, repress, deny and lie about our feelings. For example, when asked how we feel, most of us will reply—fine or—good, even if that is not true. Often, people will also say that they are not angry or not defensive, when it is obvious that they are.

Children start out emotionally honest. They express their true feelings freely and spontaneously. But the training to be emotionally dishonest begins at an early age. Parents and teachers frequently encourage or even demand that children speak or act in ways which are inconsistent with the child ‘s true feelings. The child is told to smile when actually she is sad. She is told to apologize when she feels no regret.   She is told to say—thank you, when she feels no appreciation. She is told to—stop complaining ‖ when she feels mistreated. She may be told to kiss people goodnight when she would never do so voluntarily. She may be told it is —rude ‖and—selfish‖ to protest being forced to act in ways which go against her feelings. As children become adolescents, they begin to think more for themselves. They begin to speak out more,

—talk back more and challenge the adults around them. If these adults feel threatened, they are likely to defend themselves by invalidating the adolescent 's feelings and perceptions. There is also peer pressure to conform to the group norms. Through all of this the child and adolescent learn they can 't be honest with their feelings. They gradually stop being emotionally honest with their parents, their teachers, them friends and even themselves. They learn it just doesn't 't pay to be express one's true feelings.

A Few More Thoughts On Emotional Honesty
- ✓ Dishonesty requires more energy than emotional honesty.
- ✓ When we are emotionally dis-honest we lose out on the value of our natural feelings.
- ✓ When we are emotionally dishonest, we are going against the forces of evolution rather than in harmony with them.
- ✓ It takes energy to oppose reality, nature and evolution.
- ✓ Emotional dishonesty, in authenticity and falseness create distrust and tension in society.

Comment: Honesty is one of the prized values of mankind. Honesty is an insurance against failure and defame. An honest man is a big asset to the family, to the organization and to the society in general. The honest person may not earn riches bu the will certainly earn name and satisfaction of living a good life.

<u>5.10</u> MORAL LEADERSHIP

Engineers provide many types of leadership in the development and implementation of technology, as managers, entrepreneurs, consultants, academics and officials of the government. Moral leadership is not merely the dominance by a group. It means adopting reasonable means to motivate the groups to achieve morally desirable goals. This leadership presents the engineers with many challenges to their moral principles.

Moral leadership is essentially required for the engineers, for the reasons listed as follows:

1. It is leading a group of people towards the achievement of global and objectives. The goals as well as the means are to be moral. For example, Hitler and Stalin were leaders, but only in an instrumental sense and certainly not on moral sense.
2. The leadership shall direct and motivate the group to move through morally desirable ways.
3. They lead by thinking ahead in time, and morally creative towards new applications, extension and putting values into practice. 'Morally creative' means the identification of the most important values as applicable to the situation, bringing clarity within the groups through proper communication, and putting those values into practice.
4. They sustain professional interest, among social diversity and cross-disciplinary complexity. They contribute to the professional societies, their professions, and to their communities. The moral leadership in engineering is manifested in leadership within the professional societies. The professional societies provide a forum for communication, and canvassing for change within and by groups.

5. *Voluntarism*: Another important avenue for providing moral leadership within communities, by the engineers is to promote services without fee or at reduced fees (pro bono) to the needy groups. The professional societies can also promote such activities among the engineers. This type of voluntarism (or philanthropy) has been in practice in the fields of medicine, law and education. But many of the engineers are not self-employed as in the case of physicians and lawyers. The business institutions are encouraged to contribute a percentage of their services as free or at concessional rates for charitable purposes.

6. *Community service*: This is another platform for the engineers to exhibit their moral leadership. The engineers can help in guiding, organizing, and stimulating the community towards morally- and environmentally- desirable goals. The corporate organizations have come forward to adopt villages and execute many social welfare schemes, towards this objective.

The Codes of Ethics promote and sustain the ethical environment and assist in achieving the ethical goals in the following manner:

1. It creates an environment in a profession, where ethical behavior is the basic criterion.
2. It guides and reminds the person as to how to act, in any given situation.
3. It provides support to the individual, who is being pressurized or tortured by a superior or employer, to behave unethically.
4. Apart from professional societies, companies and universities have framed their own codes of ethics, based on the individual circumstances and specific mission of the organizations. These codes of conduct help in employees' awareness of ethical issues, establish, and nurture a strong corporate ethical culture.

5.11 CODE OF CONDUCT

a. Conduct means the standard of behavior based on moral principles.
b. It is similar to code of ethics.
c. Is a management tool in setting out organization values, responsibilities and ethical obligations.
d. It provides guidance for handling difficult ethical situations.
e. Code of conduct varies from organization to organization 357

CORPORATE SOCIAL RESPONSIBILITY

f. Corporate social responsibility is the continuing commitment of corporate businesses to behave ethically and to contribute towards the welfare of the society.
g. CSR requires the companies to acknowledge that they should be publicly accountable not only for their financial performance but also their social and environmentalrecord.358
h. Corporate social responsibility.

i. It is the responsibility of corporations to go above and beyond what law requires them to do.
j. It is the responsibility to contribute to a better society and cleaner environment.
k. It is a part of corporate governance ensuring socially responsible business 359

Benefits of CSR:

l. Increased employee loyalty and retention
m. Increased quality of products and services
n. Increased customer loyalty
o. Increased reputation and brand image360

QUESTION BANK
UNIT-1 (ENGINEERING ETHICS)

1. Define Ethics? (May-08,09,Dec-10)
- Study of right or wrong.
- Good and evil.
- Obligations &rights.
- Justice.
- Social & Political deals.

2. Define Engineering Ethics? (Dec-10)
- Study of the moral issues and decisions confronting individuals and organizations engaged in engineering / profession.
- Study of related questions about the moral ideals, character, policies and relationships of people and corporations involved in technological activity.
- Moral standards / values and system of morals.

3. Differentiate Moral and Ethics? (May-08,Dec-08) MORAL:
- Refers only to personal behavior.
- Refers to any aspect of human action.
- Social conventions about right or wrong conduct.

ETHICS:
- Involves defining, analyzing, evaluating and resolving moral problems and developing moral criteria to guide human behaviour.
- Critical reflection on what one does and why one does it.
- Refers only to professional behavior.

4. What is the method used to solve an Ethical problem?
- Recognizing a problem or its need.
- Gathering information and defining the problem to be solved or goal to be achieved.
- Generating alternative solutions or methods to achieve the goal.
- Evaluate benefits and costs of alternate solutions.
- Decision making &optimization.
- Implementing the best solution.

5. What are the Senses of Engineering Ethics? (Dec-09)
- An activity and area of inquiry.
- Ethical problems, issues and controversies.
- Particular set of beliefs, attitudes and habits.
- Morally correct.

6. Differentiate Micro-ethics and Macro-ethics?

Micro-ethics: Deals about some typical and everyday problems which play an important role in the field of engineering and in the profession of an engineer.

Macro-ethics: Deals with all the societal problems which are unknown and suddenly burst out on a regional or national level.

7. Define Moral Autonomy? (Dec-10)

- Self-determining
- Independent
- Personal Involvement
- Exercised based on the moral concern for other people and recognition of good moral reasons

8. Give the importance of Lawrence Kohlberg"s and Carol Gilligan"s theory? (Dec-08) Kohlberg gives greater emphasis to recognizing rights and abstract universal rules. Gilligan stresses the importance of maintaining personal relationships based on mutual caring.

9. Differentiate Self-respect and Self-esteem?

Self-respect: It is a moral concept; refers to the virtue properly valuing oneself.

Self-esteem: It is a psychological concept; means having a positive attitude toward oneself, even if the attitude is excessive or otherwise unwarranted.

10. What are the senses of Responsibility? (May-11)

- A virtue
- Obligations
- General moral capacities of people
- Liabilities and accountability for actions
- Blameworthiness or praise worthiness

11. What are the types of Theories about Morality?

- Virtue ethics – Virtues and vices
- Utilitarianism – Most good for the most people
- Duty ethics – Duties to respect people
- Rights ethics – Human rights

12. Differentiate Hypothetical imperatives and Moral imperatives?

Hypothetical imperatives are based on some conditions whereas Moral imperatives wont based on some condition.

13. State Rawl"s principles?(Dec-12)

- Each person is entitled to the most extensive amount of liberty compatible with an equal amount for others.
- Differences in social power and economic benefits are justified only when they are likely to benefit everyone, including members of the most disadvantaged groups.

14. Give the drawbacks of Utilitarianism?

- Sometimes what is best for the community as a whole is bad for certain individuals in the community.
- It is often impossible to know in advance which decision will lead to the most good.

15. Give the drawback of Duty Ethics?

Duty ethics does not always lead to a solution which maximizes the public good.

16.   Differentiate Ethical Relativism and Ethical Egoism?(Dec-11)

Ethical egoism – the view that right action consist in producing one's own good.

Ethical relativism – the view that right action is merely what the law and customs of one's society require.

17.   Define Ethical Pluralism?

Ethical pluralism is the view that there may be alternative moral perspectives that are reasonable, but no one of which must be accepted completely by all rational and morally concerned persons.

18.   What do you mean by normative ethics?

Normative ethics deals with the professional codes of ethics that specify role norms or obligations that professions attempt to enforce. It is the recommendations of standards and guidelines for morally right or good behavior.

19.   What do you mean by ethical subjectivism?

Ethical subjectivism argues that what is ethically right or wrong for the individual depends on the ethical principles he/she has chosen. In other words, for people who subscribe to ethical subjectivism what is ethically right or wrong is entirely a personnel matter.

20.   What is tacit-ethic and Meta -ethics?

- Tacit ethic deals with the unsaid or unspoken rule of practice.
- Meta-ethics deals with theories about ethics.

PART-B

1. Explain three levels of moral development with respect to Kohlberg and Gilligan views. (Understanding) (Dec-2010, 2011) (May/June 2012) (May/June 2009) (May/June2013)
2. Discuss briefly on Ethical Theory of Right Action. Differentiate Act and Rule Utilitarian. (Creating) (Dec-2010)
3. What is Moral Dilemma? Explain the various causes of moral dilemma. (Remembering) (Nov/Dec2013)
4. Define Morality. Explain the various moral issues (Remembering)
5. Define moral Autonomy. Explain the steps that confronting moral dilemma with its causes. (Remembering)
6. Discuss different models of professional roles and explain about the consensus and controversy (Creating)
7. Define spirituality and discuss the role of spirituality in commercial organizations. (Remembering) (Nov/Dec2011)
8. Discuss the models of professional roles. (Creating)(May/June 2009) (Dec2014)
9. Explain the scopes of engineering ethics. (Understanding) (May/June2013)
10. Discuss the   importance   of   duty   ethics and   virtues in   engineering profession. (Creating)(May/June2013)
11. Detail about the senses or dimension of engineering ethics.
12. Summarize the types of inquiries. (Understanding) (Dec2014)
13. What is consensus and controversy? Brief the importance of consensus while considering moral autonomy in engineering ethics. Bring out the relationship between moral autonomy and respect for autonomy. (Remembering)
14. Explain in detail about profession and professionalism. (Understanding)

15. Explain the various types of specific virtues. Write notes on professional ideals. (Understanding)
16. How did Gilligan view the three levels of moral development initiated by Kohlberg? (Remembering) (Dec2014)
17. What are the uses of ethical theories? (Remembering)
18. Explain the skills needed to handle problems about moral issues in engineering ethics. (Understanding) (Dec2014)

PART-A

UNIT-2 (ENGINEERING AS SOCIAL EXPERIMENTATION)

1. What are the conditions required to define a valid consent?

- The consent was given voluntarily.

- The consent was based on the information that rational person would want, together with any other information requested, presented to them in understandable form.

- The consenter was competent to process the information and make rational decisions.

2. What are the two main elements which are included to understand informed consent? (May-08)

Informed Consent is understood as including two main elements:

- Knowledge [Subjects should be given not only the information they request, but all the information needed to make a reasonable decision].

- Voluntariness [Subjects must enter into the experiment without being subjected to force, fraud, or deception].

3. What are the general features of morally responsible engineers? (May-10,11)

- Conscientiousness.
- Comprehensive perspective.
- Autonomy.
- Accountability.

4. What is the purpose of various types of standards?

- Accuracy in measurement, inter changeability, ease of handling.
- Prevention of injury, death and loss of income or property.
- Fair value of price.
- Competence in carrying out tasks.
- Sound design, ease of communications.

96

• Freedom from interference.

5. Define Code?

Code is a set of standards and laws.

6. Enumerate the roles of codes? (Dec-12)

* Inspiration and Guidance

* Support

* Deterrence and Discipline

* Education and Mutual Understanding

* Contributing to the Profession 's Public Image

* Protecting the Status Quo

* Promoting Business Interests

7. Give the limitations of codes?

* Á Codes are restricted to general and vague wording.

* Á Codes can't give a solution or method for solving the internal conflicts.

* Á Codes cannot serve as the final moral authority for professional conduct.

8. What are the problems with the law in engineering?

* Minimal compliance

* Many laws are without enforce able sanctions.

9. What is the need to view engineering projects as experiments?

* Any project is carried out in partial ignorance.

* The final outcomes of engineering projects, like those of experiments, are generally uncertain.

* Effective engineering relies upon knowledge gained about products before and after they leave the factory – knowledge needed for improving current products and creating better ones.

10.   Differentiate scientific experiments and engineering projects?

Scientific experiments are conducted to gain new knowledge, while —engineering projects are experiments that are not necessarily designed to produce very much knowledgeǁ.

11.   What are the uncertainties occur in the model designs?

- Model used for the design calculations.

- Exact characteristics of the materials purchased.

- Constancies of materials used for processing and fabrication.

- Nature of the pressure, the finished product will encounter.

12.   Comment on the importance of learning from the past, using Titanic disaster, as an example?

The Titanic lacked a sufficient number of lifeboats.

13.   Comment on the importance of learning from the past, using the nuclear reactor accident at Three Mile Island, as an example?

Values are notorious for being among the least reliable components of hydraulic systems. It was a pressure relief valve, and lack of definitive information regarding its open or shut state. Similar Malfunctions had occurred with the identical values on nuclear reactors because of the same reasons at other locations, but no attention had been given to them

14.   Give any two prominent features of contemporary engineering practice that differentiate casual influence and moral accountability in engineering? (Dec-11)

- Large-scale engineering projects involve fragmentation of work.

- Due to the fragmentation of the work, the accountability will spread widely within an organization.

- There is frequently pressure to move on to a new project before the current one has been operating long enough to be observed carefully.

- The contagion of malpractice suits currently afflicting the medical profession is carrying over into engineering.

15.   Are SRBs inherently too dangerous to use on manned spacecraft? If so, why are they part of the design?

Yes, since they have the disadvantage that once the fuel is lit, there is no way to turn the booster of for even to control the amount of thrust produced. SRBs were used instead of safer liquid fueled boosters because they required a much smaller research-and-development effort. Numerous other design changes were made to reduce the level of research and development required.

16.   Under what conditions would you say it is safe to launch a shuttle without an escape mechanism for the crew?

- Have given valid consent

- Instead of rubber, steel billets for O-rings

- Liquid fueled boosters instead of Solid rocket boosters

- Design specifications 310F

17.   **In your opinion, was the Right for informed consent" of the astronauts of Space Shuttle Challenger respected?**

18.   **Define Ethical Conventionalism?**

Ethical conventionalism is the view that a particular set of conventions, customs, or laws is self-certifying and not to be questioned as long as it is the set-in force at a given time or for a given place.

19.   **State Babylon"s Building Code?**

If a builder has built a house for a man and has not made his work sound, and the house which he has built has fallen down and so caused the death of the householder, that builder shall be put to death. If it causes the death of the householder 's son, they shall put the builder's son to death. If it causes the death of the householder 's slave, he shall give slave for slave to the house holder. If it destroys property he shall replace anything it has destroyed; and because he has not made sound the house which he has built and it has fallen down, he shall rebuild the house which has fallen down from his own property. If a builder has built a house for a man and does not make this work perfect and the wall bulges, that builder shall put that wall into sound condition at his own cost.

20.   **Mention some universally accepted ethical principles (May-09, Dec-10)**

- Honesty

- Integrity

- Fulfilling commitments

- Abiding by agreements in both letter and spirit

- Willing to admit mistakes

- Being caring and compassionate

- Having respect for human dignity

PART-B

1. What are the moral and ethical lessons learnt from the space shuttle challenger study? (May/June 2012), (Nov/Dec 2013) (Remembering)

2. Explain the role of engineering projects as the experiments. (Understanding)

3. What is code of ethics? What are the positive roles of code of ethics and specify its limitation? (Dec-2010) (Remembering)

4. Compare and contrast engineering experiments with standard experiments. (Dec 2014) (Evaluating)

5. Discuss engineers as responsible experimenters. (Dec-2010) (May/June2013) (Creating)

6. Explain how moral leadership and ethical work culture influence the ethical behavior of commercial organizations (Nov/Dec 2011) (Understanding)

7. Explain as to how far there is congruence between the professional and environmental ethics. (Nov/Dec 2011) (Understanding)

8. Describethe internal and external responsibility of engineers. (May/June 2012) (Understanding)

9. Discuss the limitations of codes from engineering experimentation point of view. (Nov/Dec 2013) (Creating)

10. Compare and contrast moral values. What are the three types of values? State and explain the various attempts to reduce morality to those types of values with examples. (May/June 2009) (Analyzing)

11. What are the greater details applied to engineer project as conceived as social experiment? Given the codes play all the roles which function are the most valuable and which should be emphasized and encouraged. Why? (May/June2009)

12. Given an account of the challenger disaster and examine how the principal actors in this tragedy behaved as responsible experimenters within the framework of the engineering as experimentation model. (May/June 2009) (Dec 2014) (Remembering)

13. Write on industrial standards. (May/June 2013) (Remembering)

14. The moral responsibility of engineers should go beyond merely following the lawsǁ. Discuss (Analyzing)

15. Discuss on the roles played by the codes of ethics set by professional societies. (Dec 2014) (Creating)

PART-A

UNIT-3 (ENGINEER"S RESPONSIBILITY FOR SAFETY)

1. Define Risk? (May-09)

    a. A risk is the potential that something unwanted and harmful may occur.

Risk = Probability X Consequences.

2. What are the factors for safety and risk? Dec-08,10,11

- Voluntary and Involuntary risk
- Short-term and Long-term risk
- Expected probability
- Reversible effects
- Threshold levels to risk
- Delayed or Immediate risk etc.,

3. What are the drawbacks in the definition of Lawrence? (May-09)

- Underestimation of risks
- Overestimation of risks
- No estimation of risks

4. Give the categories of Risk?

- Low consequence, Low probability (which can be ignored)
- Low consequence, High probability
- High consequence, Low probability
- High consequence, High probability

5. What are the factors that affect Risk Acceptability? (May-12)

- Voluntarism and control
- Effect of information on risk assessment

- Job related pressures

- Magnitude and proximity of the people facing risk

6. What is the knowledge required to assess the risk?

- Data in design

- Uncertainties in design

- Testing for safety

- Analytical testing

- Risk-benefit analysis

7. What are the analytical methods? May (08)

- Scenario analysis

- Failure modes & effect analysis

- Fault tree analysis

- Event tree analysis etc.

8. What are the three conditions referred as safe exit?

- Assure when a product fails it will fail safely.

- Assure that the product can be abandoned safely.

- Assure that the user can safely escape the product.

9. How will an engineer assess the safety?

- The risks connected to a project or product must be identified.

- The purposes of the project or product must be identified and ranked in importance.

- Costs of reducing risks must be estimated.

- The costs must be weighed against both organizational goals and degrees of acceptability of risks to clients and the public.

- The project or product must be tested and then either carried out or manufactured.

10.   What are the reasons for Risk-Benefit Analysis?
   a. Risk-benefit analysis is concerned with the advisability of undertaking a project.

   b. It helps in deciding which design has greater advantages.

   c. It assists the engineers to identify a particular design score higher with that of the another one.

11. **Are the engineers responsible to educate the public for safe operation of the equipment? How?**

    a. Yes, as per the engineers are concerned with they should have their duty as to protect for the safety and wellbeing of the general public. Analyzing the risk and safety aspects of their designs can do this.

12. **Define Safety? (Dec-10)**

    a. In the definition stated by William W. Lawrence safety is defined, as a thing is safe if its risks are acceptable. A thing is safe with respect to a given person or group, at a given time, if its risk is fully known, if those risks would be judged acceptable, in light of settled value principles. In the view of objective, safety is a matter of how people would find risks acceptable or unacceptable.

13. **What is the definition of risks?(May-11)**

    a. A risk is the potential that something unwanted and harmful may occur. Risk is the possibility of suffering harm or loss. It is also defined as the probability of a specified level of hazardous consequences, being realized. Hence Risk(R)is the product of Probability (P) and consequence (C) (i.e) R = P *C

14. **Define Acceptability of risks?**

    a. A risk is acceptable when those affected are generally no longer apprehensive about it. Doubtfulness depends mainly on how the people take the risk or how people perceive it.

15. **What are the positive uncertainties in determining risks?**

    a. There are three positive uncertainties. They are:

    b. Purpose of designing

    c. Application of the product

    d. Materials and the skill used for producing the product.

16. **Define Risk-Benefit Analysis? (Dec-08)**

    a. Risk benefit analysis is a method that helps the engineers to analyze the risk in a project and to determine whether a project should be implemented or not. In risk benefit analysis, the risks and benefits of a product are allotted to money amounts, and the most benefitable ratio between risks and benefits is calculated.

17. **What does Strict Liability mean?**

a. Strict liability means if the sold product is defective; the manufacturer concerned is liable for any harm that results to users. Negligible is not at all an issue based.

18.   What is the main barrier to educational attempts?

a. An important barrier to educational attempt is that people belief changes slow and are extra ordinarily resistant to new information.

11. What happens to the products that are not safe?

Products that are not safe incur secondary costs to the manufacturer beyond the primary costs that must also be taken into account costs associated with warranty expenses, loss of customer will and even loss of customers and so.

12. What was the problem in the Chernobyl reactor?

The problem was that,

i. The output was maintained to satisfy an unexpected demand.

ii. The control device was not properly reprogrammed to maintain power at the required level.

iii.   Instead of leaving fifteen control rods as required, the operators raised almost all control rods because at the low power level, the fuel had become poisoned.

PART-B

1. Explain Risk Benefit analysis and Risk Management. (Dec-2010) (Dec 2014) (Understanding)

2. What are the factors that caused Chernobyl accident and discuss the concept of safety exist in the Chernobyl case studies (May/June 2013) (Dec 2014) (Remembering)?

3. Give a detailed discussion on safety and risk, cost and price (Remembering)

4. What are the factors that cause the nuclear accident of Three Mile Island? (Remembering)

5. Explain the role of corporate culture in ethical decision making (Nov/Dec 2011) (Understanding)

6. Explain the role of ethics and values in developing software (Nov/Dec 2011)(Understanding)

7. When no judgments about Risks are made? Explain the assessment of Risk and Safety method. (May/June 2012) (May/June 2013)(Analyzing)

8. Explain the personal risk and public risk with examples. Suggest suitable safety precautions based on the three miles case study. (May/June 2009) (Understanding)

9. How shall be the government regulator's approach to risk? (May/June 2013)
(Remembering)

10.   Explain in detail the effect of information on risk assessment with an example.
(Dec 2014) (Understanding)

11.   Discuss in detail about the Bhopal disaster case study (Analyzing)

PART-A

UNIT-4 (RESPONSIBILITIES AND RIGHTS)

1. Define Collegiality (Dec-10,11)

Collegiality is a kind of connectedness grounded in respect for professional expertise and in a commitment to the goals and values of the profession and collegiality includes a disposition to support and cooperate with one 's colleagues.

2. What are the central elements of collegiality?

a. Respect

b. Commitment

c. Connectedness

d. Cooperation

3. What are the two senses of Loyalty? (Dec-09)

i. Agency Loyalty – Acting to fulfill one's contractual duties to an employer. It's a matter of actions, whatever its motives.

ii. Identification Loyalty – Has as much as to do with attitudes, emotions, and a sense of personal identity as it does with actions.

4. When may an Identification Loyalty be said as obligatory?

i. Employees must see some of their own important goals as met by and through a group in which they participate.

ii. Employees must be treated fairly, each receiving his or her share of benefits and burdens.

5. What is the relationship between the Loyalty to the company and Professional responsibility to the public?

i. Acting on professional commitments to the public can be a more effective way to serve a company than a mere willingness to follow company orders.

ii. Loyalty to companies or their current owners should not be equated with merely obey in gone's immediate supervisor.

iii. An engineer might have professional obligations to both an employer and to the public that reinforce rather than contradict each other.

6. Define Institutional Authority? (May-08)

Institutional Authority is acquired, exercised and defined within organizations. It may be defined as the institutional right given to a person to exercise power based on the resources of the institution.

7. Define Expert Authority?

Expert authority is the possession of special knowledge, skill or competence to perform task or give sound advice.

8. What is the basic moral task of salaried engineers?

The basic moral task of salaried engineers is to be aware of their obligations to obey employers on one hand and to protect and serve the public and clients of the other.

9. What are the guidelines to reach an agreement?

a. Attack problem and not people.

b. Build trust.

c. Start with a discussion and analysis of interests, concerns, needs. It begin with interests, not positions or solutions.

d. Listen.

e. Brainstorm; suggesting an idea does not mean one aggress with it. Develop multiple options.

f. Use objective criteria whenever possible. Agree on how something will be measured.

10.   What are the essential elements of IPR?

a. Patents

b. Copyrights

c. Trademarks

d. Trade secrets

11.   What are the criteria for identifying that information is "labelled" confidential at the workplace?

a. Engineers shall treat information coming to them in the course of their as confidential.

b. Identify any information which if it became known would cause harm to the corporation or client.

c. Confidential information is any information that the employer or client would like to have kept secret in order to compete effectively against business rivals.

12. What are the terms associated with Confidentiality? (Dec-12)

a. Privileged Information

b. Proprietary Information

c. Patents

d. Trade secrets

13. How will you justify the obligation of confidentiality?

a. The obligation of confidentiality can be justified at two levels. FIRST Level : Moral Considerations
b. Respect for autonomy Respect for promises
c. Regard for public well-being SECOND Level : Major Ethical Theories
d. Rights Ethicists Duty Ethicists Rule-utilitarians Act-utilitarians

14. Define Conflicts of Interest? (May-10)

Conflict of interests is a situation in which two or more interests are not simultaneously realizable. It is the disagreement between public obligation and self-interest of an official.

15. Why does a conflict of interests arise?

a. Financial Investments

b. Insider Trading

c. Bribe

d. Gifts

e. Kickbacks

16. What is a Bribe?

A Bribe is a substantial amount of money or goods offered beyond a stated business contract with the aim of winning an advantage in gaining or keeping the contract.

17. What is called „White-collar crime"?

Occupational crimes are illegal acts made possible through one's lawful employment. It is the secret violation of laws regulating work activities. When committed by office workers of professionals, occupational crime is called _white-collar crime'.

18. What is called Kickbacks?

Prearranged payments made by contractors to companies or their representatives in exchange for contracts actually granted are called kickbacks.

19.   What are the types of Conflicts of interest?

a. Actual conflict of interest

b. Potential conflict of interest

c. Apparent conflict of interest

20.   How will you solve the Conflict problems?

a. Finding the creative middle way.

b. Employing Lower-level considerations.

c. Making the hard choice.

PART-B

1. Discuss on collegiality and loyalty. (Dec2014)(Understanding)

2. What is meant by loyalty? What are the two senses of loyalty? Is loyalty obligatory? Explain the relationship between professional responsibility and loyalty to employers(May/June2012) (Remembering)

3. Discuss human rights and professional rights in an engineering field. (Dec2014)(Analyzing)

4. Explain with case studies the four widely applicable principles of conflict resolution.(Nov/Dec 2013)

5. How far the respect for authority be recognized by salaried professionals as being morally justified? Discuss. (Nov/Dec 2013)(Remembering)

6. Explain the collective bargaining with its roles and occupational crime. (Dec-2010) (May/June 2013) (Dec2014)(Understanding)

7. How will you apply confidentiality for avoiding harmful conflicts of interests in work place? (May/June 2013)(Remembering)

8. Summarize on IPR. (May/June 2013)(Understanding)

9. What is a conflict of interest? Explain the different types of conflicts of interest with suitable examples. (Remembering)(Remembering)

10. What is meant by respect for authority? Describe in detail how institutional authority differs from expert authority.(Remembering)

11. What is meant by discrimination? Discuss your experience of some situation where you are discriminated.(Remembering)

12. Discuss in detail the various basic rights of an engineer.(Remembering)

13. Write in detail about the employee rights.(Remembering)

14. What is Intellectual Property Rights? Explain various elements of IPR in detail. (Dec 2014) (Remembering)

PART-A

UNIT-5 (GLOBAL ISSUES)

1. What are global issues?(May-08,09)

The social and environment aspects of engineer's profession and also the international context of engineering is called global issues. The global issues involve engineers as social experimenters.

2. What are the three versions of Relativism?

a. Ethical Relativism
b. Descriptive Relativism
c. Moral Relativism

3. Differentiate between technology transfer and appropriate technology.

The process by which technology is shifted to a novel setting and its subsequent implementation is called technology transfer. Whereas the process by which the suitable technology is properly identified, transferred and implemented in a new set of an environment is called appropriate technology.

4. Give any ten International rights suggested by Donaldson?(Dec-10)

a. The right to freedom of physical movement.

b. The right to ownership of property.

c. The right to freedom from torture.

d. The right to a fair trial.

e. The right to non-discriminatory treatment.

f. The right to physical security.

g. The right to freedom of speech and association.

h. The right to minimal education.

i. The right to political participation.

5. What are the reasons for the disaster at Bhopal? (Dec-10)

a. The tanks used to store Methyl Iso-cyanate were overloaded to a tune of 75%.

b. The emergency plant was also filled with a large amount of chemicals.

c. The entire refrigeration unit had been shut-down as a measure to reduce the cost and this led to increase of temperatures to a higher level.

d. One of the disappointed workers unscrewed a pressure gauge on a tank and inserted a hosepipe into it, knowing that it would cause damage, but not to this extent.

e. Scrubber has also been shutdown.

f. Flare tower was also not in an operating condition.

g. Unfortunately, there were no emergency drills or evacuation plants available.

6. What is the important concept of environmental ethics?

The new branch of applied ethics which is associated with the restoration of natural environment in a balanced state by not harming the human society through vast industrialization is called environmental ethics.

7. What are the characteristic features of human-centered environmental ethics?

The conservation of natural resources for the benefit of present and future generations and the strong emphasis on the human awareness on the destruction of nature are the characteristic features of human-centered environmental ethics.

8. What is embezzlement? (Dec-10)

The process of committing computer crimes such as stealing or cheating clients and consumers and conspiracy in the fraudulent uses of computer networks is called embezzlement.

9. How engineers justify their involvements in weapons works?

A steady and constant source of income for the livelihood of their families, better job promotional avenues with an enhanced salary and compulsive reservations in mental attitude are the primary factors with which engineers justify and compromise themselves to work defense industries.

10. What are the problems of Defense industry?

a) Problem of waste and huge cost in implementing and maintaining a weapons system.

b) Problem of Technology creep.

c) Problems in maintaining secrecy.

d) Every country allocates large amount of its resources to defense sector [India spent ¼ of its resource for defense]

11. **What is an ethical climate?(May-11)**

The favorable and workable atmosphere that is essential for the responsible conduct of an engineer is called ethical climate. This ethical climate enables engineers to contribute their maximum best to their corporate companies.

12. **What are the special features of an ethical corporate climate?**

a. Ethical values are widely appreciated by managers and employees.

b. A corporate code of ethics is emphasized for using ethical language.

c. Moral tone is set up in policies by management by providing suitable guidelines for professional codes of ethics.

d. Proper methods and procedures for conflict resolution are suitably evolved.

PART-B

1. Explain the code of ethics specified by IEEE and ASCE. (May/June2013)(Understanding)

2. Discuss on computer, business and environmental ethics? (Dec-2010) (Dec 2014)(Creating)

3. Discuss an engineer's involvement in weapons work. (May/June 2013) (Dec 2014)(Creating)

4. Explain the code of ethics specified by ASME and IETE.(Understanding)

5. Explain the process of creating an ethical organization.(Nov/Dec 2011)(Understanding)

6. Discuss the role of media in promoting ethical practices among business. (Nov/Dec 2011) (Creating)

7. Define Technology transfer. Why engineers to study computer ethics? Explain the customer relation to computer ethics and the importance of computer ethics. (May/June 2012) (Understanding)

8. Define the following concepts. i) Biocentric ethics ii) eucentric ethics iii) sentient center ethics. (May/June 2012)(Remembering)

9. State an illustrative case study that touches upon some fundamental issues in environmental ethics. (Nov/Dec 2013)(Remembering)

10. Do engineers have a moral right to carry out what they consider to be unethical activity? Explain in detail with a case study. (Nov/Dec 2013)(Analyzing)

11. What do environmental ethics deal with? Discuss the holistic approach of environmental ethics. Write a note on acid rain. (May/June 2009)(Remembering)

12.   What are the reasons for selecting engineers as managers? How to maintain the ethical climate in organization? List the principles for conflict resolution and how to solve the conflicts through the managerial approach.(May/June2009)(Dec 2014)(Remembering)

13.   Discuss the ethical issues related to computer and internet. (May/June 2013) (Dec 2014)(Creating)

14.   Differentiate honesty and moral leadership. (May/June2013)

15.   Discuss the different forms of relativism with respect to MNCs (Creating)

16.   Explain the role of engineers as consultant (Understanding)

17.   Discuss the role of engineers as expert witness and advisors. (Dec 2014)(Creating)

UNIT V AND UNIT VI

1. Give an account of Bhopal Gas Tragedy.

OnDecember3,1984, Union Carbide's pesticide-manufacturing plant in Bhopal, India leaked 40 tons of the deadly gas, methyl isocyanate into a sleeping, impoverished community -killing 2,500 within a few days, 10000 permanently disabled and injuring 100,000 people. Ten years later, it increased to 4000 to 7000 deaths and injuries to600,000.

Risks taken:

    a. Storage tank of Methyl Isocyanate gas was filled to *more than 75%* capacity as against Union Carbide's spec. that it should *never be more than 60%* full.

    b. The company's West Virginia plant was controlling the safety systems and *detected leakages thro' computers* but the Bhopal plant *only used manual labor for control and leak detection.*

    c. The Methyl Isocyanate gas, being highly concentrated, *burns parts of body* with which it comes into contact, even *blinding eyes and destroying lungs.*

Causal Factors:

- Three protective systems *out of service*

- Plant was *understaffed* due to costs.

- Very *high inventory of MIC*, an extremely toxic material.

- The accident occurred in the *early morning.*

- Most of the people killed lived in a shanty (poorly built) town located very close to the plant fence.

Workers made the following attempts to save the plant:

- They tried to turn on the plant refrigeration system to cool down the environment and slow the reaction. (*The refrigeration system had been drained of coolant weeks before and never refilled -- it cost too much.*)

- They tried to route expanding gases to a neighboring tank. (*The tank's pressure gauge was broken and indicated the tank was full when it was really empty.*)

- They tried to purge the gases through a scrubber. (*The scrubber was designed for flow rates, temperatures and pressures that were a fraction of what was by this time escaping from the tank. The scrubber was as a result in effective.*)

- They tried to route the gases through a flare tower -- to burn them away. (*The supply line to the flare tower was broken and hadn't been replaced.*)

- They tried to spray water on the gases and have them settle to the ground—by this time the chemical reaction was nearly completed. (*The gases were escaping at a point 120 feet above ground; the hoses were designed to shoot water up to 100 feet into the air.*)

In just 2 hours the chemicals escaped to form a deadly cloud over hundreds of thousands of people incl. poor migrant laborer's who stayed close to the plant.

> ***2.** What are the benefits of Multi-National corporations doing business in less developed countries for both the MNCs and the host country?*

Benefits to MNCs:

- ☐ *a. Inexpensive labour*
- ☐ *b. Availability of natural resources*
- ☐ *c. Favorable tax conditions*
- ☐ *d. Fresh markets for products*

Benefits to developing host countries:

- ☐ *a. New jobs*
- ☐ *b. Greater pay and greater challenge*
- ☐ *c. Transfer of advanced technology*
- ☐ *d. Social benefits from sharing wealth*

3. What are the three senses of relative values?

3.1. Ethical Relativism

- *Actions are morally right in a particular society if they are approved by law, custom, or other conventions of the society.*

3.2. Descriptive Relativism

- *Value beliefs and attitudes differ from culture to culture and this is a fact.*

3.3. *Moral Rationalism or Contextualism (Ethical pluralism)*

- *Moral judgements should be made in relation to factors that vary between issues. Hence it is not possible to formulate rules that are simple and applicably to all situations.*

4. Which standards should guide engineers' conduct when working in foreign countries?

a. *Alternate 1: 'When in Rome, do as the Romans do'*
b. *Alternate 2. Follow the identical practices which were followed in the home country.*
c. *Both are unacceptable. A via media should be found based on the context.*

5. What are the International Rights as enumerated by Thomas Donaldson?

- *The right to freedom of physical movement*

- *The right to ownership of property*

- *The right to freedom from torture*

- *The right to a fair deal*

- *The right to non-discriminatory treatment*

- *The right to physical security*

- *The right to freedom of speech and association*

- *The right to minimal education*

- *The right to political participation*

- *The right to subsistence*

6. What can MNCs do to promote morally just measures? Or what are Richard T. De George's guidelines for moral promotion by MNCs?

- *MNCs business should do more overall good than bad towards the economy of the host country than doing good to a few corrupt leaders in oppressive regimes.*

- *They must respect laws and regulations of the local country as long as they do not violate basic moral rights.*

- *They must pay a living wage, even when local companies fail to pay such a wage, but otherwise pay only enough to attract competent workers.*

- *It is permissible for the US to transfer dangerous technology like asbestos production to another country and then simply adopt that country's safety laws only under the following conditions.*

- *Workers may be so desperate for income to feed their families that they will work under almost any conditions*

- *Pay workers for the extra risk*

☐ *Good judgements exercised in good faith, than abstract principles, is the only way to address practical problems.*

7. Write in brief about Technology Transfer and Appropriate Technology?

7.1. Technology Transfer:

'The process of moving technology to a novel setting and implementing there.'

- *Novel setting is any situation containing at least one new variable relevant to success or failure of given technology*

- *Transfer of technology from a familiar to a new environment is a complex process*

7.2. Appropriate Technology:

'Identification, transfer, and implementation of the most suitable technology for a new set of conditions'

- *Conditions include social factors that go beyond routine economic and technical engineering constraints*

- *Identifying them requires attention to an array of human values and needs that may influence how a technology affects the novel situation*

- *Intermediate technology*

8. How is environment degraded?

1. *By causing injuries to nature*

   a. *Usually, this damage is caused slowly*

   b. *Sometimes this also happens in sudden strikes*

2. *Misuse of our resources, fouling our environment*

3. *Practicing growths in consumptions and population leading to non-availability of resources*

4. *Industrial activity denudes land(to destroy all plant and animal life), pollutes atmosphere and water, reduces the yield from sea and land*

9. What are the questions to be answered by Engineers in their role as experimenters?

- *How does an industry affect the environment?*

- *How far it can be controlled?*

- *Whether protective measures are available and implemented?*

- *Whether engineers can ensure safe & clean environment?*

10.   What is acid rain? What are its effects?

Acid rain:

a.   *pH of normal rain is 5.6*

b.   *pH of rainfall in north eastern areas of North America is 3.9 to 4.3. It is 10 to 100 times more acidic than normal. This is 'acid rain'.*

c.   *Snowmelt into water releases huge amount of acid which got frozen during winter.*

Effects:

a.   *Acid shock' from snowmelt causes mass destruction of fish. On long term it also harms fish eggs and sources of food.*

b.   *Thousands of lakes were killed by acid rain in Scandinavia and North America.*

c.   *The causes are burning of fossil fuels leading to release of SO2 in particular and Nitrogen oxides.*

d.   *Problems of Sweden caused by Industrial plants in England and North Europe.*

e.   *Problems of North America caused by utilities in Ohio valley, the largest polluter of SO2 in USA.*

Some of the potential changes are still unknown

- *Micro-organisms in soil are being affected*

- *Groundwater is polluted but its ultimate effects are not known*

- *The effects may be known only after another 100years Effect on food sources are also unclear*

11.   What are the other problems caused to the environment?

a.   *Build-up of CO2 from the use of fossil fuels by Industrial nations could result in Greenhouse effect.*

b.   *Damage to protective OZONE layer due to the release of Freon is related to technological products used by the people of these nations.*

12.   What is Greenhouse effect?

'Greenhouse Effect' is defined as 'The progressive warming up of earth's surface due to blanketing effect of man made CO2 in the atmosphere.'

A green house is that body which allows the short wavelength incoming solar radiation to come in, but does not allow the long wave outgoing infra red radiation to escape. The earth's atmosphere bottles up the energy of the sun and it acts like a greenhouse, where CO2 acts like a glass windows.

13.   What are the effects of Greenhouse?

☐ *a.* *The temperature effect of the CO2 and water vapor combined together has a long range impact on the global climate.*

☐ *b.* *Because of increased concentration of CO2 and due to much warmer tropical oceans, there may occur cyclones and hurricanes and early snow melt in mountains will cause more floods during monsoon.*

☐ *c.* *Increase in global temperature can adversely effect the world food production.*

☐ *d.* *At higher altitudes in the atmosphere, CO2 undergoes photochemical reactions producing CO, which is drastically dangerous.*

☐ *e.* *CFCs are responsible for 20% increase in warming. This may increase the chances of diseases in humans and animals.*

14.   Describe the case study of environmental degradation caused by PCB & Kanemi's Oil?

In Southern Japan, in 1968 a large number of people suffered by disfigurement of skin, discolouration, fatigue, numbness, respiratory distress, vomiting and loss of hair.

-    *10,000 people got affected & some died*

-    *Two groups of 121 people each were tested and results were as follows:*

  -   *It was found that fried food using rice oil produced by Kanemi company was eaten which caused the problem*

  -   *After 7 months of investigation....*

    - *It was found that the presence of Polychlorinated biphenyl-PCB was the cause for the effects and it was present in the rice oil.*

    - *RiceOilwasheatedatlowpressuretoremovetheodourthro'aheatexchanger and a liquid known as KANECHLOR which contained PCB was used for heat transfer*

    - *Pipes of the heat exchanger was corroded and led to leakage thro' those pinholes.*

    - *In fact, Kanemi had been replenishing 27 kgs of lost PCB per month for sometime without realizing the seriousness.*

Indirect path – this rice was used as chicken-feed and half of one million chickens that were fed died.

Other Similar Effects:

❖ *Plastic bakery wrappers containing PCB mixed with ground stale bread was used as chicken-feed and 140000 chickens had to be slaughtered in NewYork.*

❖ *PCB leaked into fish meal from a heating system in North Carolin a plant and 12000 tons of fishmeal were contaminated and 88000 chicken, fed with fish meal had to be destroyed.*

❖ *High pressure injection of water near Baldwin Dam in Los Angeles caused the reservoir crack open along a fault line. The water released killed 5 and damaged property worth $14million.*

15. How can we internalize Costs of Environmental Degradation?

❖ *Time cost of a product – includes numerous factors like effect of pollution, the depletion of energy and raw materials, social costs, etc.*

❖ *If these costs are internalized (added to the price), then the cost can be charged directly to the beneficiary of the degradation of environment.*

❖ *It is better to make the user to pay for all its costs than to levy higher taxes.*

❖ *An acceptable mechanism for price fixing must be found by the engineer with the help of the economist, scientist, lawyer and politician which could protect the environment through self-correcting procedures.*

❖ *Good design practices may give better environmental protection without added cost.*

16. Give a brief account of Technology Assessment?

• *Engineers are said to be finding the right answers for the wrong questions*

• *Finding the right questions is much more difficult than finding the right answers to these questions*

• *Engineers should*

  ▪ *Try to access the technology and its environmental impacts and form containing the major adverse effects*

  ▪ *During assessment even if engineers were strongly believing that projects have no adverse effect, they should continue to monitor the outcomes even after its implementation which only would give the complete picture of the consequences of the project*

17. Write short notes on Sentient – Centered Ethics, Bio – Centric Ethics, Eco centric Ethics and Human – Centered Environmental Ethics.

Sentient – Centered Ethics

Sentient animals are those which feel pain and pleasure. This version of Nature-centered ethics is advanced by some utilitarians, notably Peter Singer, who says that right action maximizing good for all should include sentient animals as well as humans. Failure to do so leads discrimination like racism, which is known as 'Speciesism'. There is always a dispute as to whether the inherent worth of animals can be equated to human beings or not.

Bio – Centric Ethics

This regards all living organisms as having inherent worth. We should live with the virtue of 'reverence to life', as set forth by Albert Schweitzer (1875-1965). This will enable us to take decisions about when life can be sacrificed.

Ecocentric Ethics

This locates inherent worth in Ecological systems and this approach is different from the other two, as it is not individualistic. This is voiced by Aldo Leopold (1887-1948). There is another view that ecocentric ethic does not replace socially generated human-oriented duties to family, neighbours and humanity

Human – Centered Environmental Ethics

This is an extension of ethical theories to combat threats to human beings presented by the destruction of nature.

18.   *Define computer ethics?*

Computer Ethics deals with 'the evaluation of and decision making in a variety of moral problems caused by computers'.

19.   *What shifts are caused in power relationships by Computers?*

Power relationship caused by Computers:

1. *Job Elimination:*

   ❖ *Computers still continue to lead to elimination of jobs.*

   ❖ *While employees cannot be paid when there is no work, all attempts are to be made by employers to readjust work assignments and retain employees.*

   ❖ *Theabsenceofthispracticecreatesanemployeeorpubicbacklashagainstintroduction of Computers.*

2. *Customer Relations:*

   ❖ *It is very easy for a customer to notice an error in a computer printout, of the price difference between what is shown at the shelf and what is shown in cash receipt register.*

❖ *Here moral sense and long term business requirement requires that the policies should be made favorable to consumers.*

3. *Biased Software:*

A group of people with known convictions, may tend to produce software which favours their views rather than views from all angles to let the user decide finally.

4. *Stock Trading:*

Automatic, hands-off trading of stocks and currency can be performed, benefiting the trading community but it will harm the intended purposes.

5. *Unrealistic Expectations:*

Sales personnel have a tendency to oversell systems that are too large for customers' requirements; sometimes even those which are not ready for delivery.

6. *Political Power:*

By obtaining information about different groups of people regarding their attitudes and values, the computers can be made to help politicians to make speeches, send mails, etc. which would be appealing selectively to these groups.

7. *Military Weapons:*

Computerized military weapons, even if perfected, will only make opposing countries to develop their striking or responding capability which is not healthy for the world.

20.   What problems are encountered in the use of computers with properties?

The two major problems encountered in the use of computers with properties are:

1. *Embezzlement and*

2. *Theft of software and information*

21.   How the problem of embezzlement takes place through computers and why?

❖ *The speed and geographic coverage of the computer system and the difficulty of tracing the transactions through computers makes catching the thieves troublesome.*

❖ *Computers are abused in i) stealing by employees at work, ii) stealing by non-employees or former employees ,iii) stealing from or cheating clients and consumers, iv) violating contracts for computer sales or service and v) conspiring to use computer networks to engage in widespread fraud.*

❖ *Penalties for computer crime are mild compared to conventional crimes.*

❖ *Passwords and more recently, data encryptions are used for security with limited effectiveness.*

22. ***Explain briefly about Data and Software with respect to property problems.***

❖ *'Data' is information stored in a computer.*

❖ *'Software' or 'program' consists of i) an algorithm, ii) a source code and iii) an object code.*

❖ *Software can be protected by Copyrights and Trade secret laws. Patenting on software is limited to detailed coding sequences but not final products. Algorithms and object codes cannot be copyrighted. But source code can be copyrighted. Eg. Buying one copy and reproducing dozens of copies*

23. ***Describe how and in what ways 'violation of privacy' occurs in and through Computers.***

Computers make more information available to more people. This makes protection of computer privacy difficult.

1. Inappropriate Access:

a. *Documents recorded for a crime which one did not commit but was arrested. As a child you were arrested for drinking alcohol*

b. *Medical data about visits to a psychiatrist. A loan default to a National Bank.*

c. *Any of the above information can be accessed by, let us say, a prospective employer during a security check.*

2. Data Bank Errors:

a. *Even erroneous information when generated by computers is taken to be authenticated.*

b. *Immediate reaction to such wrong information may mostly prove to be incorrect.*

3. Hackers:

a. *Hackers' are people who compulsively challenge any computer security system, choke networks, give out false information, etc.*

c. *This can be extremely harmful.*

d. *It is a violation of property rights.*

e. *At the least, it reduces productivity by shutting down systems.*

26. Give one argument each for and against Weapons Development?

Weapons Development *is a **defensive measure** against greater destruction by political adversaries, terrorists and enemy states.*

*They are **devices to kill** human beings, innocent civilians or equally unwilling soldiers on the other side.*

27. What should engineers do in taking part in Weapons development?

Engineers need to examine one's conscience to take part in any form of weapon development.

- o *They have to consider the circumstances leading to the specific conflict and decide whether it is justified to take part in associated weapons development.*

- o *If necessary, they should refuse to be a part of it and be prepared to face consequences.*

- o *Individual privacy, national security, freedom to protect proprietary information are three values requiring limits on access to information.*

24. How has law responded to computer abuses?

a. *A series of laws enacted to prevent abuse of information.*
b. *Information can be accessed only by consumer consent or court order.*
c. *Consumers have the right to examine and challenge information contained in computers.*

25. What Professional Issues arise in Computer ethics?

Owing to the high degree of job complexity and technical proficiency required, a lot of issues arise in engineering ethics.

1. Computer failures:

a. *Failures can occur due to either hardware or software Hardware errors do not occur frequently.*
b. *Software errors are the major failures of the computers. Hardware errors are easily detected.*
c. *Software errors are difficult to detect.*
d. *Trial runs are absolutely essential to check the program.*

2. Computer Implementation:

a. *New computer system should be attempted successfully before the old one becomes inoperative. Many failure cases have been reported while switching over to a new system.*

3. Health Conditions:

a. *Ergonomic conditions should be implemented to reduce back problems, provide wrist support, to become good looking.*

28. How much is being spent in Defence expenditure and how Arms Trade gets promoted by private manufacturers of arms?

- o *Hundreds of billions of dollars, annually, throughout the world, are being spent for military operations.*

- o *25% of this is spent on just procurement of weapons.*

- o *17% of these are spent in transactions across countries.*

<u>*Promotion of Arms Deals:*</u>

1. *Krupp, a family of successful arms merchants and manufacturers*

2. *Armies and navies invested in Krupp's nickel steel armour*

3. *Then Krupp made chrome steel shells that can pierce nickel leading to further investment by military.*

4. *Then they made a high-carbon armour plate that can resist the new shells resulting in more orders*

5. *Then Krupp again produces, 'capped shot' with explosive noses which apiece through the high-carbon armored plate also*

6. *Arms deals continued to flourish*

7. *Vickers and Schneider-another arms manufacturer*

8. *Supplying arms to Chinese, Japanese and Russians Pointing out the growth of the Japanese navy to Chinese*

9. *Pointing out the growth of the Chinese to their rivals, Russians*

10. *Russia–Japanese war in 1905 was useful for the cause of arms manufacturers. Russians lost the war, hence ordered fresh arms for rehabilitation*

11. *Japanese won the war, but were upset since terrible bloodbath was caused by Russians machine guns on land.*

29. Describe the destructive nature and power of weapons and their development?

a. *Towards the end of World War II, night raids sometimes on civilian areas were very common*

b. *The deaths caused by Atom bombs on Hiroshima, Nagasaki were not more than the deaths caused by single air raids in World War II*

c. *But they were horrible because of their power in rapid delivery of destructive power in immense concentration*

d. *Hiroshima Bomb – equivalent to 20000T of TNT powder carried on 267 bogies of railroad (2 miles long) for one bomb – again equivalent to 740-B52 bombers to carry this load.*

e. *USSR exploded Hydrogen bombs in 1960 – 50 & 60 mega ton range for tests with capabilities such as:*

    a. *2000 to 3000 times powerful than Hiroshima bomb*

    b. *4000 to 6000 miles long train required to carry an equivalent amount of TNT powder which will take 100 hours to pass any point*

    c. *Will require one and a half million planes +(bombers) to carry the powder*

    d. *Towards the end of cold war*

e. *USSRhad5800megatons(9500warheadson2700launchers)and USA had 3300 megatons (10800 warheads on 2000 launchers)*

30. Illustrate the involvement of engineers in Weapons Development with examples.

1. *Bob is employed by a firm manufacturing anti-personnel bombs. These bombs tie up much of the enemy's resources in treating the wounded who survive its explosion (by showering its fragments on to the victims). Though he does not like to be involved in bomb , he justifies himself that someone would have to mfr them. If he does not, then someone else will. Of course, his family also needs a steady income.*

2. *A chemical engineer, Mary, got in to napal mmfg when she was promoted. She does not like wars, but she feels that govt. knows better about international dangers. She also knows that if she continues doing well in her job, she will again be promoted to work on a commercial product.*

3. *Ron is a specialist in missile control and guidance. He knows that he was one of the engineers instrumental in keeping any potential enemy in check through his work. At least, there is enough mutual deterrence for a third world war.*

4. *Joanne is an electronics engineer working also on avionics for fighter planes that are sold abroad. She does not want these planes to be sold to hostile countries. Since she does not have any say on who should be their customers, she even alerts occasionally her journalist friends with information about her work which she feels all public should have.*

Anyone who is involved in weapons development should be very clear as to his/her motives for being in the industry.

31. What are the Problems of Defense Industry in brief?

1. *Large military build-ups, massive projects all lead to unethical business practices and the urgency of completion of the weapons projects does not allow proper controlling and monitoring.*

2. *'Technology creep' – development of cruise missiles alters diplomatic arrangements*

3. *The impact of secrecy surrounding any defense activity*

4. *Overall effect of defense spending on economy*

32. Explain the problems of defense industry with examples.

1. *Large military build-ups: $2 billion cost overrun on the development of C5-A cargo plane reported to the public by Ernest Fitzgerald due to poor operating efficiencies in defense industry. He pointed out how large suppliers felt secure in not complying to cost-cutting plans but small contractors were willing.*

   a. *25% firms hold 50%of all defense contracts and 8 firms conduct 45% of defense research.*

2. *Technology creep:* The arms are not only growing in size, it is also becoming better. The development of a new missile or one that can target more accurately, by one country, can upset or destabilize a diplomatic negotiation. Sometimes this fad for modernization leads to undesirably consequences. The F15 fighter planes were supposed to be fastest and most maneuverable of its kind but most were not available for service due to repairs, defects and lack of spares. Engineers should be beware of such pitfalls.

3. *Impact of secrecy:* Secrecy poses problems to engineers. Engineers should be aware of the answers to the following questions:
Should discoveries of significance to military be informed to govt.? Can they be shared with other researchers, in other countries? Should they be withheld from the scientific and public community? Will the secrecy in weapons development will also serve to hide corruption or their mistakes in defense establishments? Can secrecy help the promotion of weapons systems without criticism or interference from outsiders?

4. *Effect on economy:* Every dollar spent on defense produces less jobs than what could be provided for by using the resource on other neglected sectors such as education and road development. May be a changeover by training defense engineers to use their designs, processes and techniques to bring about better, competitive civilian products is what would be the most appropriate thing to do now.

33. What are the difficulties in Decommissioning Weapons?

1. *Even now, shells (duds or live) which landed about 90 years back during World War I are found by farmers during ploughing. Special bomb disposal squads are being kept busy with hundreds of calls.*

2. *There are, still more, unexploded and hidden bombs all over the world that fell during World War II*

3. *Severed limbs and dead bodies are being discovered inlands filled with mines in Cambodia and Vietnam in 1960sand70s.*

4. *Anti-personnel weapons are found in Afghanistan, Angola, Bosnia, Mozambique, Nicaragua and Somalia.*

5. *These weapons are easily spread by air but are very difficult and dangerous to detect and remove.*

6. *About 100 million landmines remain still scattered in the above countries as per estimates by U.S.State dept.*

7. *Land mines present a serious ethical dilemma to leaders who want to be ethical in wars also*

8. *Design, mfr, deployment and eventually their disposal is a huge experiment.*

9. *Widespread ignorance on radiation amongst the public*

10. *Gas warfare experiments, Anthrax carriers, nuclear weapons all cause both known and unknown problems*

11. *Engineers dealing with dangerous material should consider both the intended use and also the unintended consequences and also their disposal*

. 34. Which studies are more useful to 'engineer managers' than even engineering?

Richard L.Meehan, a civil engg graduate from MIT, was retained by General Electric as a consultant to testify before Nuclear Regulatory Commission about the capability of GE's nuclear plant in California, U.S.A. to withstand earthquakes.

He found, while trying to understand the effect of earthquakes on nuclear plants, that

1. *His basic study of physics is more useful in studying this area compared to the more advanced studies in engg.*
2. *His understanding of risk analysis was based not only on probability theory but also on value judgement about safety.*
3. *But more interesting was that understanding people was more important than anything else.*
4. *Person oriented skills are as important to engineers as technical skills.*

34. *Why managements prefer to make engineers as managers than non- engineers? / Why engineers find management positions attractive?*

a. *Engineers undergo the most intensive technical training amongst professionals. But still, many of them move to managerial positions early in their career for which they received no training.*
b. *Organisations find it easier to teach the business side to engineers than teaching engineering to non-engineers.*
c. *They also value the quantitative analysis, strong work- ethics, and confidence in problem solving exhibited by engineers.*
d. *Engineers also prefer the management attractive, since career in management offers better recognition than technical track.*

34. *Managers' responsibility is to conduct business to increase profits'. Discuss.*

- *Nobel laureate Milton Friedman said 'The social responsibility of business is to increase its profits……. The responsibility of managers is to conduct business in accordance with their stockholders' desires, which generally will be to make as much money as possible while conforming to he basic rules of society, both those embodied in law and those embodied in ethical custom'*

- *The ethical custom refered by Friedman means only 'refraining from fraud, deception and corruption.*

- *But Martin and Schinzinger say that Friedman is not correct in saying that managers' ethics reduce to only responsibility to maximize profits for stockholders.*

- *The primary responsibility of managers is to produce product or service while maintaining respect for persons, including customers, employees and public.*

- *Ethically, personnel and safety comes first before profits.*

- *By definition, compared to charitable institutions, religions, organizations, etc organizations and corporates operate only for profits.*

- *But the ultimate goal of managers should be to make valuable products that are also profitable since profit making is one of the conditions to be in business.*

- *Good business and sound ethics go together. Hence the moral roles of managers and engineers are complementary and not opposed.*

- *Engineermanagershavetwomajorresponsibilities–promotingandethicalclimateand resolving conflicts.*

35. Explain how Ethical Climate is promoted in organizations through examples.

There are highly ethical organizations, examples of some of which are given below:

1. *Marilyn Hamilton, founded Quickie Designs in 1980, who was a teacher and athlete who was paralyzed in hang-gliding accident. A highly mobile and versatile wheel chair was designed weighing 26 pounds, half the weight of chairs that were currently produced. The company grew up within a decade to $65 millions in sales. It had a policy of customer sponsored sports events for young people in wheel chairs. It is relatively small (500 strong) and exceptionally committed.*

2. *Martin Mariette Corpn began an ethics program in 1985 emphasizing basic value like honesty and fairness and responsibility for environment and high product quality. They drafted a code of conduct, conducted and ethics workshop for managers and created effective procedures for employees to express their ethical concerns.*

3. *Texas Instruments (TI) is an example of an ethical large corporation emphasizing on trust, respect for other persons, etc. TI appointed a full time Ethics Director, Carl Skooglund. He surveyed to know the ethical concerns of employees and their awareness. He conducted workshops on ethics, wrote brochures and was directly to all employees through a confidential phoneline. Even though they made it clear that unprofessional conduct would not be tolerated, the focus was on supporting ethical conduct than punishing wrongdoers.*

4. *A large defense contractor started an ethics program that was not successful. Higher management viewed the program as a success but the professional employees considered it as a sham/farce for public relations and window dressing. The primary difficulty was the gap between the intentions of top management and the unchanged behavior of the Senior managers.*

38. What steps can be taken to improve the ethical climate by managers?

1. *Ethical values and their full complexity are widely acknowledged and appreciated by managers and engineers. Neither profits nor promoting the interests of the*

organization is neglected but the moral limits on profit-seeking go beyond simply obeying the law and avoiding fraud.

2. *The sincere use of ethical language is recognized as a legitimate part of corporate dialogue. This is done either by formulating corporate code of ethics or by including ethical responsibilities in job descriptions at all levels.*

3. *Top management must set a moral tone, in words, in policies and by personal example. Everyone should be confident that management is serious about ethics.*

4. *There must be procedures for conflict resolution. Managers should be trained to r esolve conflicts and on the other hand, a person should be exclusively made to have confidential discussions about moral concerns.*

39. What are the most common conflicts?

o *Conflicts over schedules, depending mostly on support depts. but where managers do not have any control.*

o *Conflicts over which is the most important dept or function at a given time*

o *Conflicts over personnel resources*

o *Conflicts over technical issues*

o *Conflicts over administrative procedures*

o *Personality conflicts*

o *Conflicts over costs*

40. Can conflicts be managed by force or authority? How are different conflicts resolved?

o *'I am in-charge - see it my way or I will fire you'. This is generally perceived as self- defeating.*

o *Conflict arrangement sometimes means tolerating and even inviting some forms of conflict*

o *Manager's task is to create climate in which conflicts are addressed constructively*

o *Personality conflicts are ranked relatively low in intensity but they are most difficult to resolve.*

o *They are generally woven with technical/communication problems*

o *Properly managed technical and ethical conflicts are usually fruitful and not harmful. Differing views provide opportunity for improved creativity.*

41. What are the 4 ways to resolve conflicts among persons suggested by Harvard Negotiation Project?

1) *People: Separate people from the problem. Even though both the people and the problem are important, the personal aspect of the conflict should be separated from the problem to deal with it better. On personality clashes, the focus should be on behaviour and not on people.*

2) *Interests: Focus on interests and not position\s This principle applies most clearly to personnel matters and ethical views, rather than technical disputes. Positions are stated views but these may not really express their best interests.*

3) *Options: Generate a variety of possibilities before deciding what to do. Create a wide range of options especially in technical and ethical issues and facilitate discussions.*

4) *Criteria: Insist that the result be based on some objective standard. Beyond the goals of efficiency, quality and customer satisfaction, it is important to develop a sense of fair process in how the goals are met.*

42. What is the nature of work for Engineers as Consulting Engineers?

Consulting engineers work in private practice. They earn by getting their fee for services rendered. They have greater freedom in decision making compared to salaried employees. But they also have a need to earn a living.

43. What are the major areas of work for engineer consultants?
a. *Advertising*
b. *Competitive bidding*
c. *Contingency fees*
d. *Safety and client needs*

44. Advertising, once thought to be unprofessional has now been accepted by law' – Explain.
a. *Before 1976, advertising was thought to be 'unprofessional', in U.S.A. The state felt that work should be won through reputation as engineer and not through advertisement.*
b. *But in 1976, Supreme Court ruled that*
c. *Ban on professional advertising is an improper restraint*
d. *It reduces public awareness of available professional services*
e. *They keep prices higher than they might otherwise.*

Now the focus has been shifted to restrain deceptive advertising which is done through:

a. *Outright lies*
b. *Half-truths*
c. *Exaggeration*
d. *Making false suggestions or implications*
e. *Obfuscation (confusion or not being clear) created by ambiguity, vagueness*
f. *Manipulation of the unconscious*

45. When is advertising considered to be deceptive?

Example 1: A consulting firm played actually a very minor role in a well-known project

Situation 1: Its brochure claims that it played a major role

Situation 2: It makes no claim but only shows the picture of the project

Situation 3: It shows the picture along with a footnote in fine print the true details about its role in the project

Situation 4: If the same statement is printed in larger type and not as footnote.

Example 2: An ad shows an electronics device to convey that the item is routinely produced and available for sale. But actually the ad shows only the prototype or mock- up and the item is just being developed.

46. What are the norms to be followed by ethical consultants in advertising?

a. *Generally consumer products can be advertised suppressing the negative aspects and even some exaggeration is allowed.*
b. *But advertisement of professional services like engineering services is governed by strict norms.*

NSPE forbids the following:

"the use of statements containing a material misrepresentation of fact or omitting a material fact necessary to keep the statement from being misleading; statements intended or likely to create an unjustified expectation; statements containing prediction of future success; statements containing an opinion as to the quality of the showmanship including the use of slogans, jingles or sensational language format."

a. *Some degree of solicitation may be useful in encouraging healthy competition*
b. *Or will it open the door to people who are not honest, who criticize unfairly or who exaggerate the merits of their services?*
c. *In any case, restrictions on misleading advertisement are a must.*

47. Why was Competitive Bidding prohibited earlier and then why was it approved by courts?

* ❖ *Competitive bidding was prohibited for quite sometime due to the following reasons:*

* ❖ *Consulting jobs, unlike industrial and construction work, are not suitable for precise cost estimates and hence precise bids.*

* ❖ *Here competitive bidding, would encourage cutting safety and quality, in case of lower bids and padding/over designing in the case of higher bids.*

❖ *Later, Competitive bidding was approved by Courts of law on the reasoning that free trade is restrained in an unfair manner.*

48. When consulting engineers reject competitive bidding, what can be the basis of their selection?

Consulting engineers, in the absence of competitive bidding can be selected only based on their reputation and proven qualification. But younger, competent engineers may be disadvantaged by this method.

49. What is your understanding of Contingency Fees?

Contingency fee is dependent on some specific conditions beyond normal, satisfactory performance in work.

    a. *A client may hire a consultant engineer to find methods of cost saving on an ongoing project to save a minimum of 10%. If consultant saves 10%, he will get his fee; otherwise no fee will be paid. The fee can be either an agreed amount or a %age of savings.*

    b. *When the fee is a% age of saving, it becomes 'contingency fee'. In many cases, consultants tend to be biased and in order to gain the fee, they may specify inferior design or process to cut costs.*

50. How does NSPE address the issue of 'Contingency Fee'?

NSPE has addressed this issue as follows:

"An engineer shall not request, propose, or accept a professional commission on a contingent basis under circumstances in which his professional judgement may be compromised, or when a contingency provision is used as a device for promoting or securing a professional commission."

51. When does the 'contingency fee' become permissible?

To decide whether 'contingency fee'practice may be allowed or not,the potential gains should be weighed against the potential losses. Hence, this again calls for contextual reasoning based on ethical theories, which provide a framework for assessing morally relevant issues of the problem.

52. How 'Safety and client needs' should be addressed by consulting engineers?

❖ *Consulting engineers have greater freedom with wider areas of responsible decision making compared to salaried engineers.*

❖ *This creates special difficulties for consulting engineers.*

❖ *In 'design-only' projects, consultants do not have any role in the construction or implementation as per the design specs.*

❖ *Ideally, only the designer would really know the areas of difficulty in execution.*

❖ *Even when changes in design are required during execution, the consultant may not be around to effect the changes*

❖ *Client may not have capable people for inspection of the work based on the consultant's design.*

❖ *Does the consultant have a moral responsibility to follow through the design inexecution*

❖ *In any case, job safety is one prime responsibility of the consultant engineer*

53. What are the reasons that cause 'Disputes'? Who is the major loser in any dispute?

a. *Large projects involve owners, consultants and contractors and many participants at various levels in these three organizations.*
b. *Overlapping responsibilities, fragmented control, delays and inability to resolve disputes are some of the problems encountered during these projects.*
c. *Resolving disputes becomes especially difficult when projects last for several years and connected personnel also change during this period.*
d. *Owners have the most to lose in such situations. Hence they try to shift the risks to others.*
e. *Consulting engineers are generally tied to the contract provisions and they do not try any innovative ideas (do not want to add risks)*
f. *All this have led to considerable litigation and any litigation is time consuming and costly.*

54. What are the steps to be taken resolve disputes?

1. *Define how risks are to be apportioned and payment of fees to be made*

2. *Make contractual provisions for dispute solving vehicles to avoid legal battles in lines of mediation –arbitration*

3. *Mediator attempts to resolve first and if it fails, the arbitrators' decision should be final.*

4. *National Joint Board for settlement of Jurisdictional Disputes will be called to provide a leaking board and appeals board.*

5. *The Consulting Engineer, from the "social experimentation" nature of engineering, has the obligation to include such clauses in contracts and should make sure that these clauses are adhered to by all.*

55. What is the work done by Engineers as Experts?

Engineers, in their position as experts, explain the happenings of the past in terms of Causes of accidents, malfunctions of equipment and other technological events. They also help in events of the future like, public planning, potential of patents and policy making (in technology)

56. How should Expert Engineers function?

They should function as impartial seekers of facts & Communicators of truth but not as hired guns i.e. advocates for lawyers, officials, etc

57. What are the types of cases, expert witnesses are called upon to testify in court & what are the stakes?

57.1. *Types Of Cases*

I. *Airplane crash*

II. *Defective products*

III. *Personal injury*

IV. *Property damage*

V. *Traffic accident*

57.2. *Stakes*

I. *Legal liabilities*

II. *Economic interests*

III. *Reputations of corporations and professionals*

58. What are the Expert engineers' responsibilities towards their hirers?

They should

- *Present their qualifications to the client*

- *Investigate thoroughly the cases entrusted to them.*

- *Testify in court*

59. How should the expert witness exhibit one's 'confidentiality responsibility'?

The expert witnesses must

✓ *Not divulge their investigations unless called upon to do so by the court*

✓ *Not volunteer evidence favorable to the opponent*

✓ *Answer questions truthfully when opposing attorney puts forth pertinent questions But he should not just be the client's mouthpiece.*

60. What are the aims of a legal system?

Aims Of A Legal System is

To administer a complex system of legal rights that define legal justice achieved through adversarial relationships, with rules about admissible forms of evidence and permissible forms of testimony

61. What is the role of an expert in a court system consistent with Professional standards (codes of ethics)?

Role of an Expert in a Court System

✓ _Experts must earnestly try to be impartial in identifying and interpreting complicated data thrown up by the complexity of modern science and technology to help the courts_

✓ _Ideally, if courts pay the expert witness, the expert will become totally unbiased._

✓ _But it is a very costly issue_

✓ _So parties to the dispute are called upon to pay and hire them on both sides and also allow them to be cross examined by both sides_

62. What is the difference between Eye witness and Expert witness?

- _Eye Witness Is permitted to testify on observed and to some extent perceived facts._

- _Expert Witness Is permitted to testify on facts, perceptions and interpretations off acts in the area of their expertise comment on opponent's expert witness' view report on applicable professional standards_

63. What are the types of abuses of Engineers as Expert witnesses?

Expert witnesses are abused in the following ways:

✓ _Hired Guns_

✓ _Financial Bias_

✓ _Ego Bias_

✓ _Sympathy Bias_

64. Write short notes on: a) Hired Guns, b) Financial Bias, c) Ego Bias and d) Sympathy Bias

a) _Hired Gun An unscrupulous (unprincipled, crooked, immoral) engineer_

- _Makes his living by helping lawyers to portray facts in favour of their clients_

- _Never tries to be objective_

- _Violates standards of honesty and care in conducting investigations_

- _Overall a shame on engineering community) Financial Bias_

    ✓ _The expert witness is biased to the party which pays more money_

✓ *The bias increases substantially when payments are agreed as Contingency Fee to be paid only in case the hirer wins the case*

✓ *Full time forensic engineers, being dependent on lawyers for their living, try to create a reputation of a winning engineer.*

<u>c)</u> *Ego Bias*

✓ *Competitive attitudes, being on one side of the disputing parties makes an expert, egoistic and makes him influence judgments*

✓ *They start identifying themselves with their side of the dispute <u>d) Sympathy Bias</u>*

✓ *The plight of the victims and their sufferings can invoke sympathy from the expert witness*

✓ *This upsets impartial investigation of facts*

65. What is needed of the Expert Engineers?

✓ *Engineer Experts should maintain their integrity in the face of all the above biases*

✓ *Courts also must rely on balance provided by expert witnesses on both sides of the case and provide opportunities to lawyers to remove the bias by cross-examination*

66. What is the work of Engineers as Advisers?

Engineers act as Advisers in Planning and Policy-Making like Economists, sociologists, urban planners, etc.

In Policy-Making they advise about the Cost benefit analysis of alternate solutions for transport, housing, energy, defense, etc.

In Planning they check the feasibility, risks and benefits of the specific technological projects which affect public in local communities

67. What are the Stakes for the engineer advisers?

Their stakes are:

1. *Opposing political views*

2. *Social perspectives*

3. *Economic interests*

4. *And their individual values like,*

5. *Honesty*

6. *Public trust*

7. *Respect for common good*

68. How should Engineer advisers act?

Advisers are to:

- ✓ *Chart all realistic options*
- ✓ *Carefully assess each under different assumptions about future contingencies*
- ✓ *Act favourable to the client by basing their studies on particular assumptions about future contingencies*

69. What are the factors that influence Advisers?

Advisers are influenced by:

- ✓ *Large amounts of money involved*
- ✓ *Direct and overt (obvious and unconcealed) pressure applied by pro or anti-people involved in that project*
- ✓ *Hope of additional work in future*
- ✓ *Their wish to get the respect of clients*

70. What are the normative models of Advisers? Briefly explain each of them.

Normative Models of Advisers

Three types:

- ▪ *Hired Guns*
- ▪ *Value Neutral Analysts*
- ▪ *Value Guided Analysts*

Hired Guns – This is the most undesirable role that can be played by the adviser.

- ✓ *Here the obligation to clients only is paramount and other values are not bothered about.*
- ✓ *Studies are made just conforming to the client's wish.*
- ✓ *Adviser highlights only the favourable facts to the customer.*
- ✓ *All the unfavourable facts are very much downplayed.*

Value Neutral Analysts

- ✓ *Completely impartial engineers.*
- ✓ *They identify all options and analyze factual issues of each option.*
- ✓ *Cost-benefit analysis are made based on value criteria specified and made public*

Value Guided Analysts

✓ *Responsibility to public paramount*

✓ *Maintain honesty about technical facts and values*

✓ *They can adopt partisan views for the good based on their professional judgment*

71. What are the virtues of independent expert advisers?

<u>Virtues of Independent Experts</u>

✓ *Honesty-* *avoiding deception, being candid in stating relevant facts and truthful in interpreting facts*

✓ *Competence- being well trained, adequately experienced in the relevant field and having relevant skills*

✓ *Diligence- carrying out tasks carefully and promptly*

✓ *Loyalty- avoiding conflicts of interest, maintaining confidentiality and concern for the interests of the client*

72. List the roles of engineers as 'leaders'.

Engineers perform as <u>Leaders </u>in the roles of

1. *Managers*

2. *Business Entrepreneurs*

3. *Consultants*

4. *Academics and*

5. *Govt officials.*

73. What is leadership and who are moral leaders?

Leadership is 'Successfully moving a group towards its common goal'.

*But Moral leaders are those who move the group successfully towards goals which do public good and not evils i.e. the goals must be 'morally valuable'. Hence **Moral Leaders** can be defined as,*

'The individuals, who direct, motivate, organize, creatively manage and move groups toward morally valuable goals'

74. 'Technologists were best qualified to govern because of their technical expertise'. Discuss in detail.

Mussolini and Hitler were great leaders, but not 'Moral Leaders', since their goals were not morally valuable.

'An Utopian society shall be governed by a philosopher-king whose moral wisdom best qualifies him to rule' – <u>Plato</u>

'Technologists were best qualified to govern because of their technical expertise, as well as their logical, practical and unprejudiced minds'– <u>Frederick Taylor</u>

   a. *But no single profession has the only right to moral governance of society.*
   b. *Leadership is also moving away from any narrow professional interests.*
   c. *Moral leadership is not' dominance by elite', but stimulating groups toward morally desirable ends.*

75. Explain Moral Creativity.

Moral creativity is

   a. *Identifying most important values in particular situations*
   b. *Focusing on them through effective communication within the group. Deep commitments grounded in integrity to implement them.*
   c. *Creativity consists in identifying new possibilities for applying, extending and putting into practice, rather than inventing values.*

76. How participation in Professional Societies will improve moral leadership?

Professional Societies

   o *Promote continuing education for their members*

   o *Unify the profession, speak and act on behalf of them*

   o *Are a forum for communicating, organizing and mobilizing change within, a change which has a moral dimension.*

   o *Cannot take any pro-employee or pro-management stand since they have members in management, supervision and non-management.*

   o *But they can play a role in resolving moral issues*

   o *A moral responsibility as well as moral creativity is shared.*

77. How can individuals make a difference in leadership of Professional Societies?

   o *Stephen H. Unger, as an individual was mainly responsible for persuading IEEE to focus on supporting responsible engineers than punishing wrong doers. He was instrumental in IEEE presenting awards to the three BART engineers.*

   o *In 1988, NSPE created National Institute of Engineering Ethics with a mission to promote ethics within engineering. The focus was on education rather than propaganda.*

   o *But effective professional activity, requires a substantial trust from clients and the public.*

o *Building and sustaining that trust is an important responsibility shared by all engineers.*

o *In this area also Moral Leadership within professional societies is important.*

78. Write short note on 'Leadership in Communities'.

Leadership responsibilities of engineers as citizens go beyond those of non- engineers. They should provide greater leadership in social debates about Industrial Pollution Automobile Safety Disposal of Nuclear Waste, etc.

79. What are the different views on 'leadership in communities'?

a. *One view is that no one is strictly obligated to participate in public decision making. It may be a moral ideal for citizens.*

b. *An opposite view is that all are obligated to devote sometime and energy in public policy making*

c. *Non-engineers should at least stay informed about public issues and professionals have obligations as experts in their areas.*

d. *Hence the need for identifying and expanding areas of possible good.*

80. What are the arguments for and against Voluntary Service by engineering professionals?

a. *Should engineering professionals offer engineering services to the needy, without charging fee or at reduced fee?*

b. *Voluntarism of this kind is already encouraged in Medicine, Law and Education.*

c. *But ABET code states "Engineers shall not undertake or agree to perform any engineering service on a free basis" and other codes also insist that engineers are obligated to adequate compensations (which means full fee)*

d. *Engineers find it difficult to donate their services individually compared to doctors and lawyers since their output is on a shared basis*

e. *But, as suggested by Robert Baum, engineers can volunteer their services in the following areas, in groups, either free or at cheaper than normal fee.*

f. *Environmental impact studies that is harmful to a community Health issues of polluted water and soil*

g. *Minimal needs of elderly and minorities like running water, sewage systems, electric power and inexpensive transportation.*

81. What can engineers and engineering society do to public in terms of 'voluntary service'?

Engineers can

a. *Urge Govt. to expand services of the Army Corps of Engineers*

b. *Encourage students to focus their projects on service for disadvantaged groups*

c. *Encouraging corporations to cut their fee by 5 to 10% for charitable purposes.*

Morally concerned Engineering Profession-

> a. *Should recognize the rights of corporations and engineers to voluntarily engage in philanthropic engineering services.*
> b. *Professional societies should endorse voluntary exercise as a desirable ideal.*

Many engineers and some societies already are engaged in

> a. *Tutoring disadvantaged students*
> b. *Advice local governments on their engineering problem.*

References

1. *Mike W Martin and Roland Schinzinger, Ethics in Engineering,4th edition, Tata McGraw Hill Publishing Company Pvt Ltd, New Delhi,2014.*
2. *Charles D Fleddermann, Engineering Ethics, Pearson Education/ Prentice Hall of India, New Jersey,2004.*
3. *Charles E Harris, Michael S Protchard and Michael J Rabins, Engineering Ethics- Concepts and cases, Wadsworth Thompson Learning, United states,2005.*

4. *http://www.slideword.org/slidestag.aspx/human-values-and-Professional-ethics.*

5. *M Govindarajan, S Natarajan and V S Senthil Kumar, Engineering Ethics, PHI Learning Private Ltd, New Delhi,2012.*

6.*R S Naagarazan, A text book on professional ethics and human values, New age international (P) limited ,New Delhi,2006.*

More
Books!

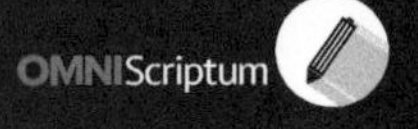

OMNIScriptum

Printed by Books on Demand GmbH, Norderstedt / Germany